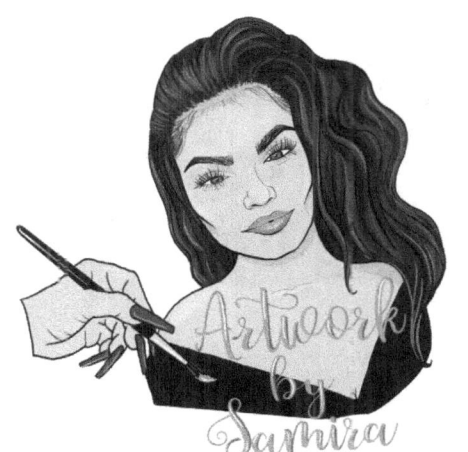

Thank you for supporting my business!

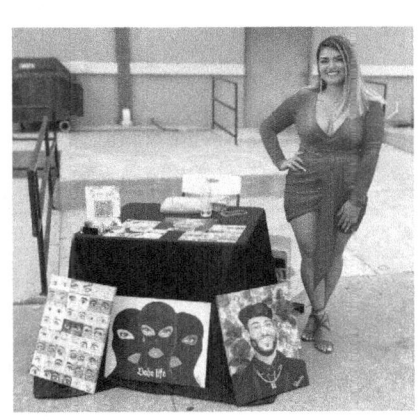

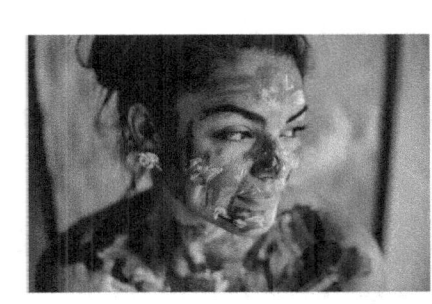

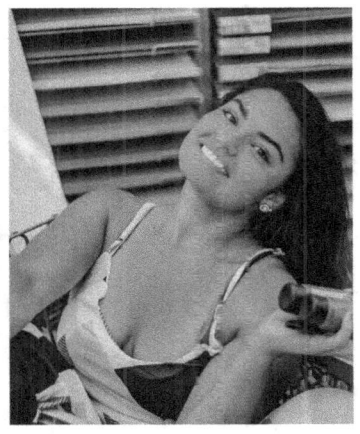

Connect with me!

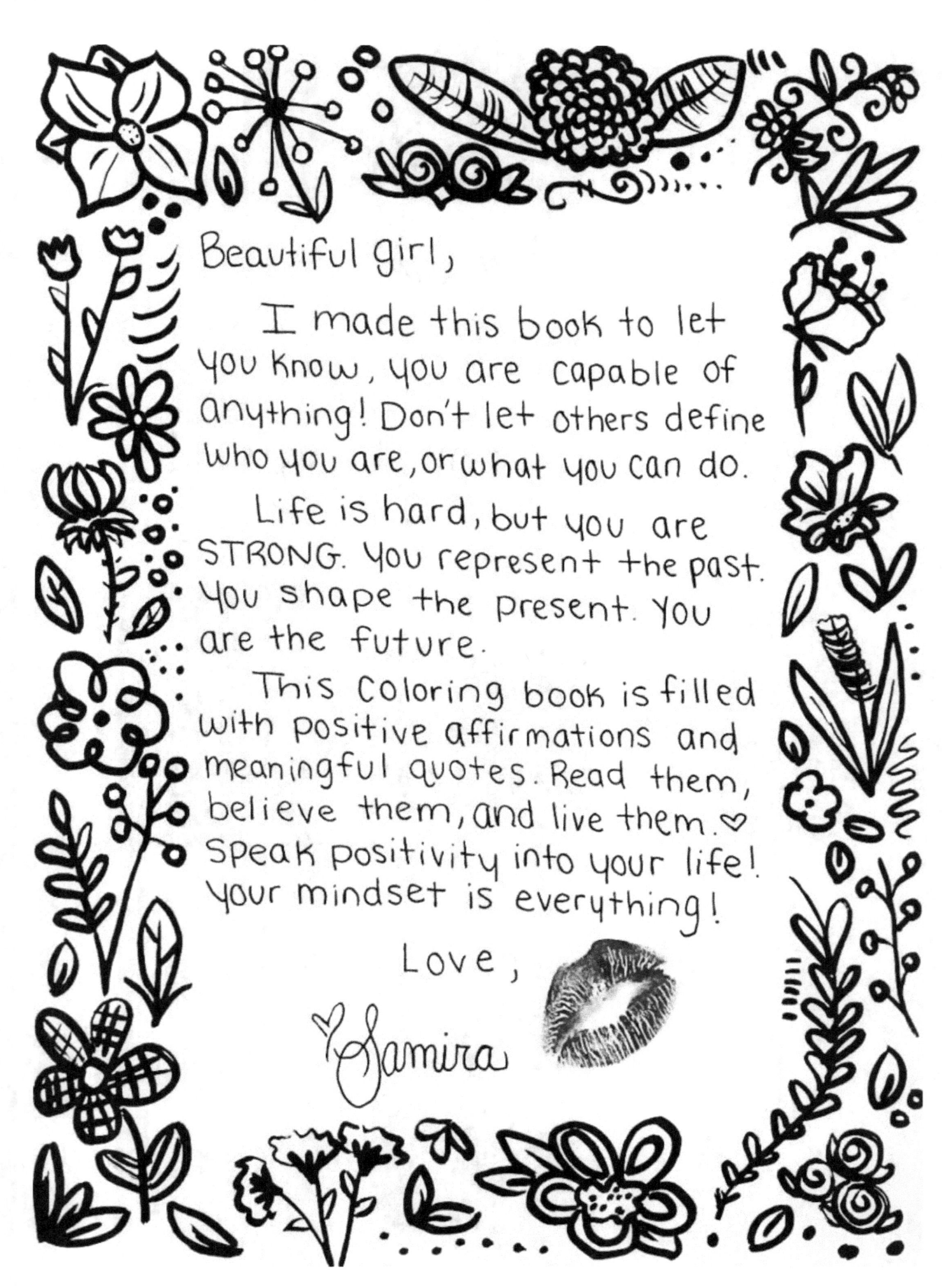

Beautiful girl,

I made this book to let you know, you are capable of anything! Don't let others define who you are, or what you can do.

Life is hard, but you are STRONG. You represent the past. You shape the present. You are the future.

This coloring book is filled with positive affirmations and meaningful quotes. Read them, believe them, and live them. ♡ Speak positivity into your life! Your mindset is everything!

Love,

♡ Samira

What is a positive affirmation?

A positive affirmation is a phrase or sentence you say as if it is already true, or on its way to becoming true.

You describe how you want to be (or what you want to accomplish) in a way that affirms that it is already true. Positive affirmations are a piece of what makes up the "growth mindset" idea.

Examples:

Original Statement	Positive Version
"I hope I pass this test."	"I am smart enough to pass this test."
"I made a mistake."	"I learn from my mistakes."
"I can't do it; I'm afraid."	"I'm brave enough to try."

What can I do with positive affirmations?

❖ Read them out loud
❖ Pick three that fit you and repeat them to yourself throughout the day, or when you have negative thoughts.
❖ Write down some on sticky notes, and put them on your mirror as a daily reminder.
❖ Tear out your coloring page and frame it.
❖ Help a friend by sharing some positivity with them. (With any of the affirmations in this book, you can change the word "I" to "you") Example: If your friend says she feels sad, you can tell her, "You are brave. You got this!" or you could tell her, "You are strong enough to conquer this problem!"
❖ Pick one positive affirmation to focus on for the day or week, and talk to your family (or parents talk to your children) about changes you noticed.
❖ Change your phone screen to an affirmation for a subconscious reminder!
❖ Write some positive words to a friend or family member to encourage them.
❖ Create your own affirmations that are specific to your life.

My mental health

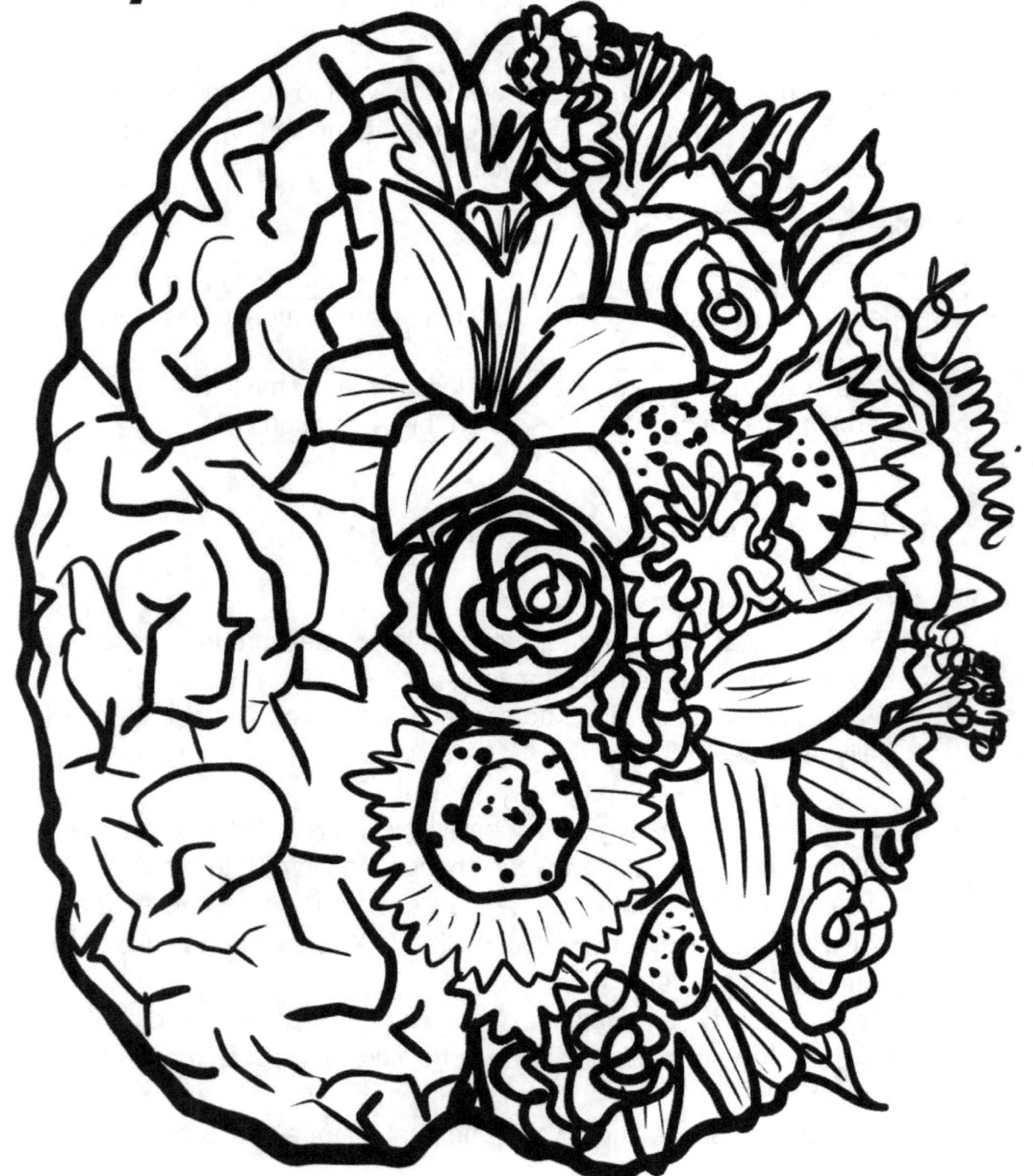

is just as important as
my physical health

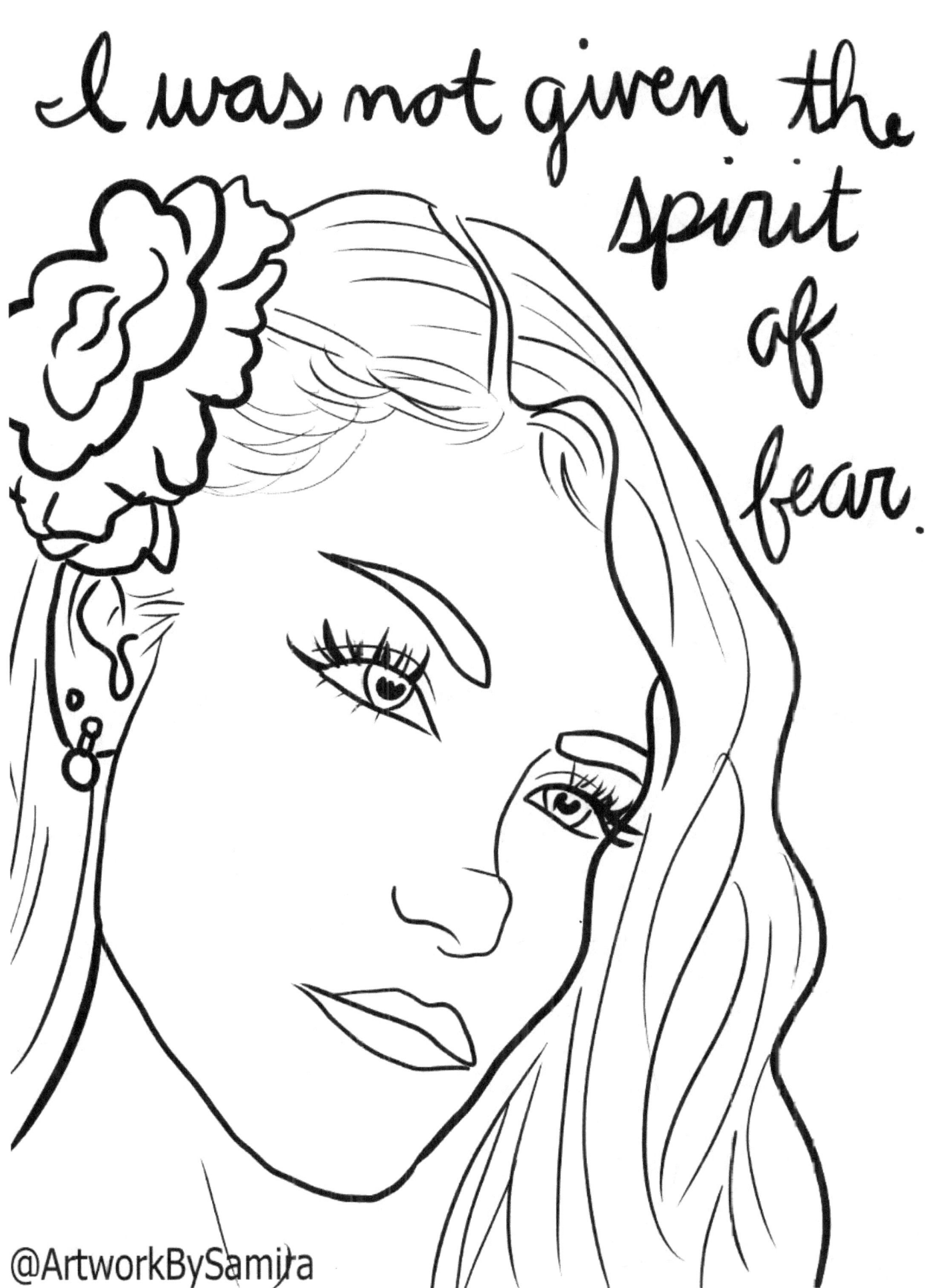

I was not given the spirit of fear.

@ArtworkBySamira

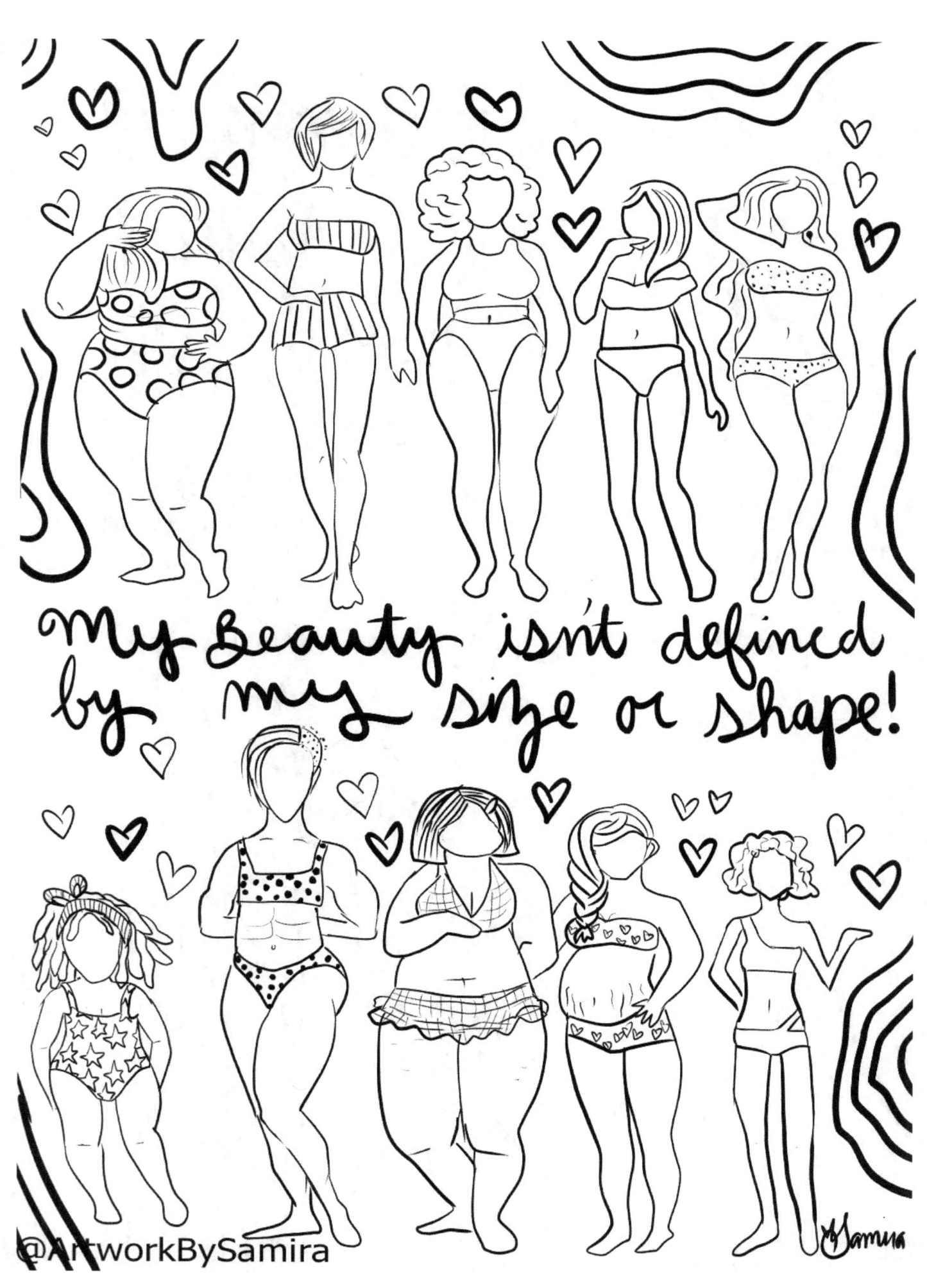

My Beauty isn't defined by my size or shape!

@ArtworkBySamira

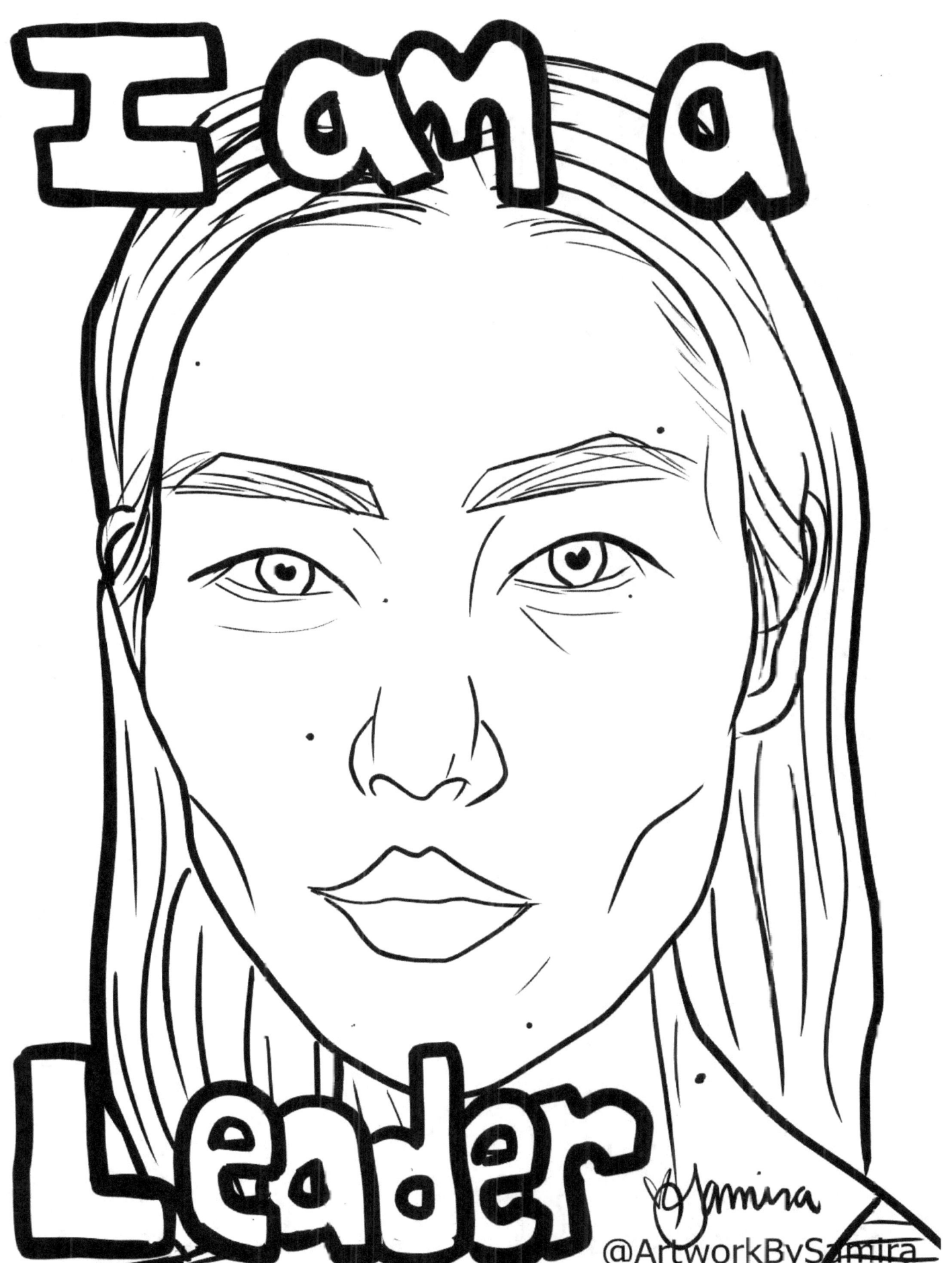

I am a

Leader

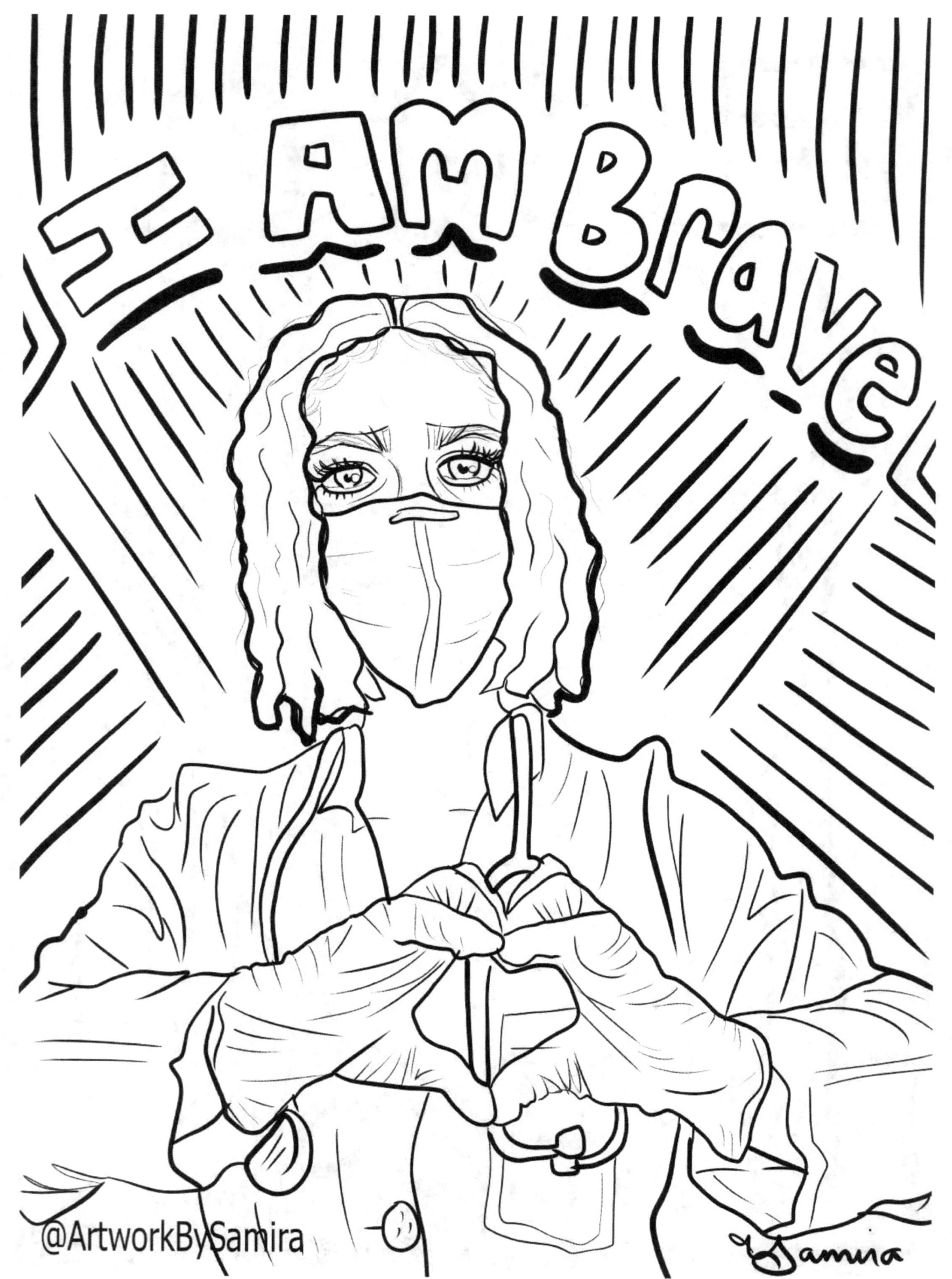

Do something today that your future self will thank you for.

Samira

I was born with a PURPOSE

@ArtworkBySamira

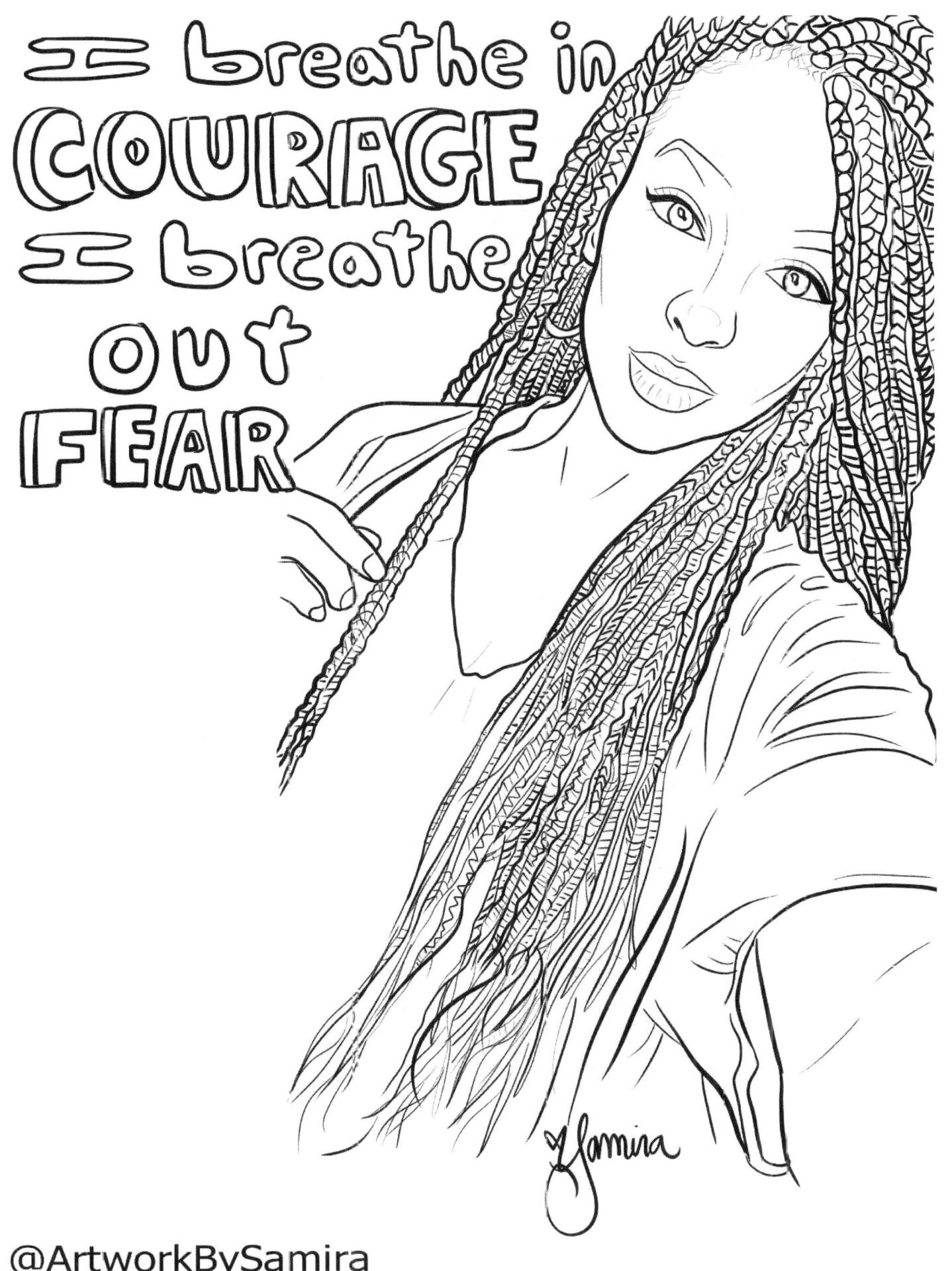

@ArtworkBySamira

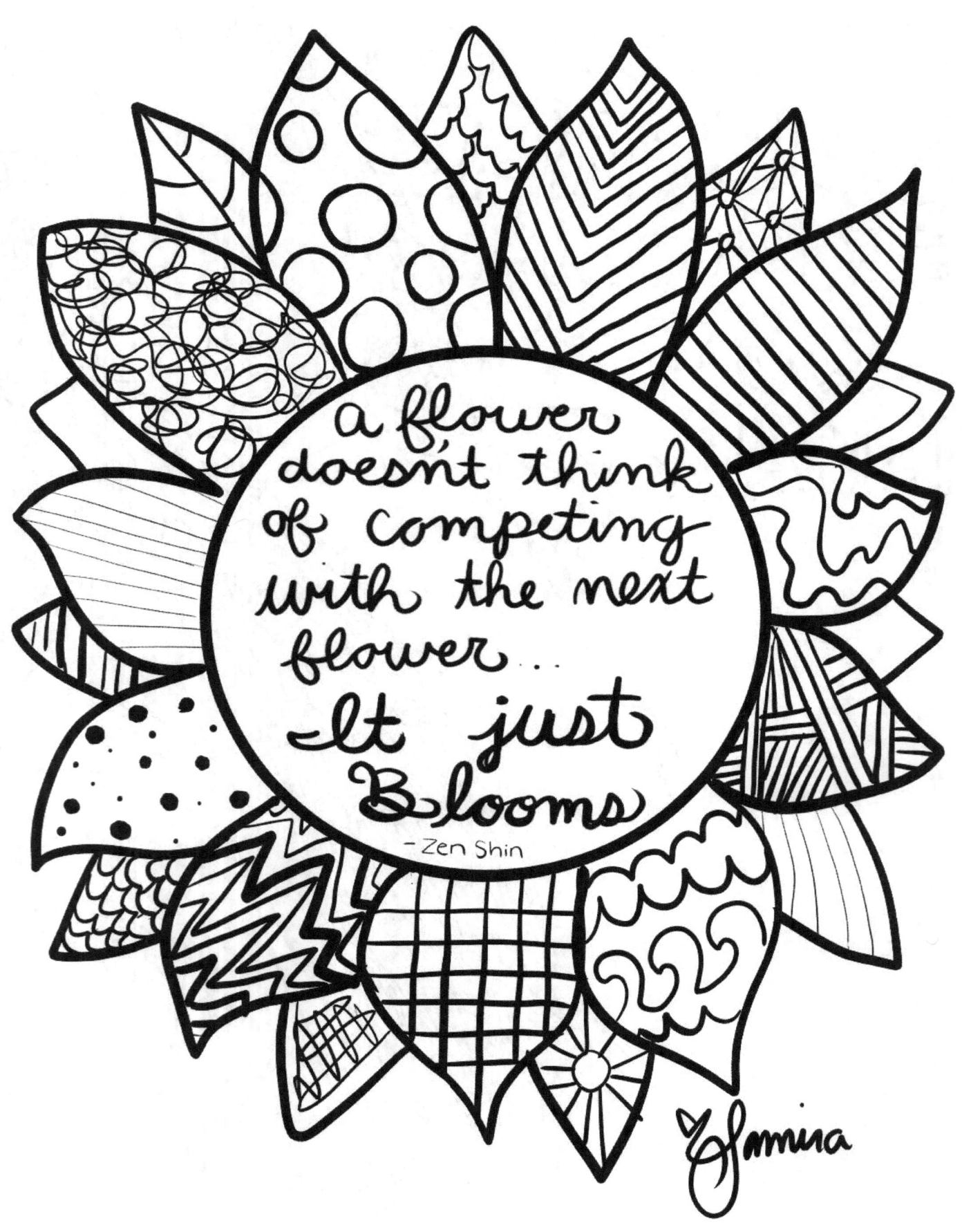

a flower doesn't think of competing with the next flower... It just Blooms
- Zen Shin

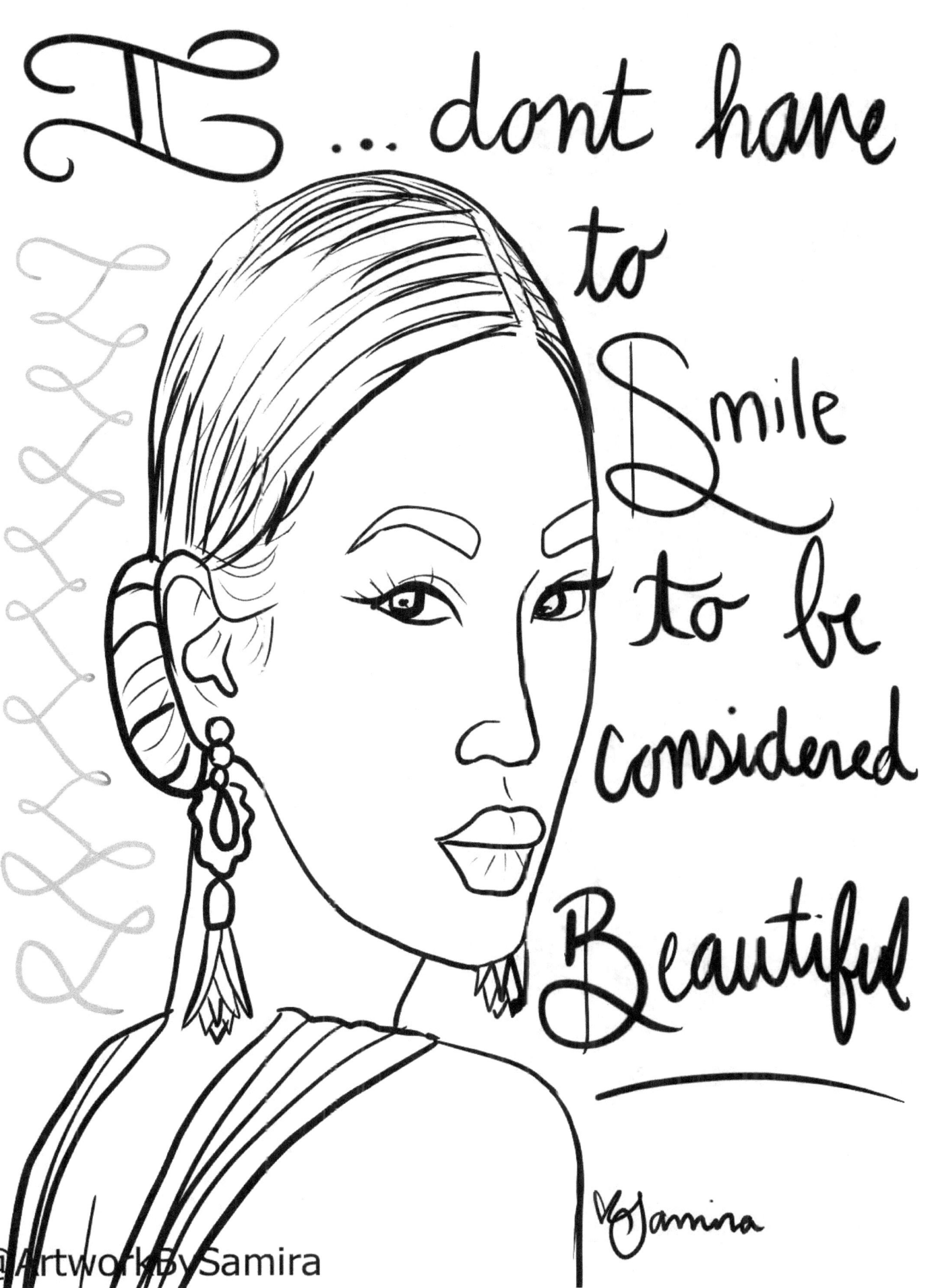

I ... dont have to Smile to be considered Beautiful

@ArtworkBySamira

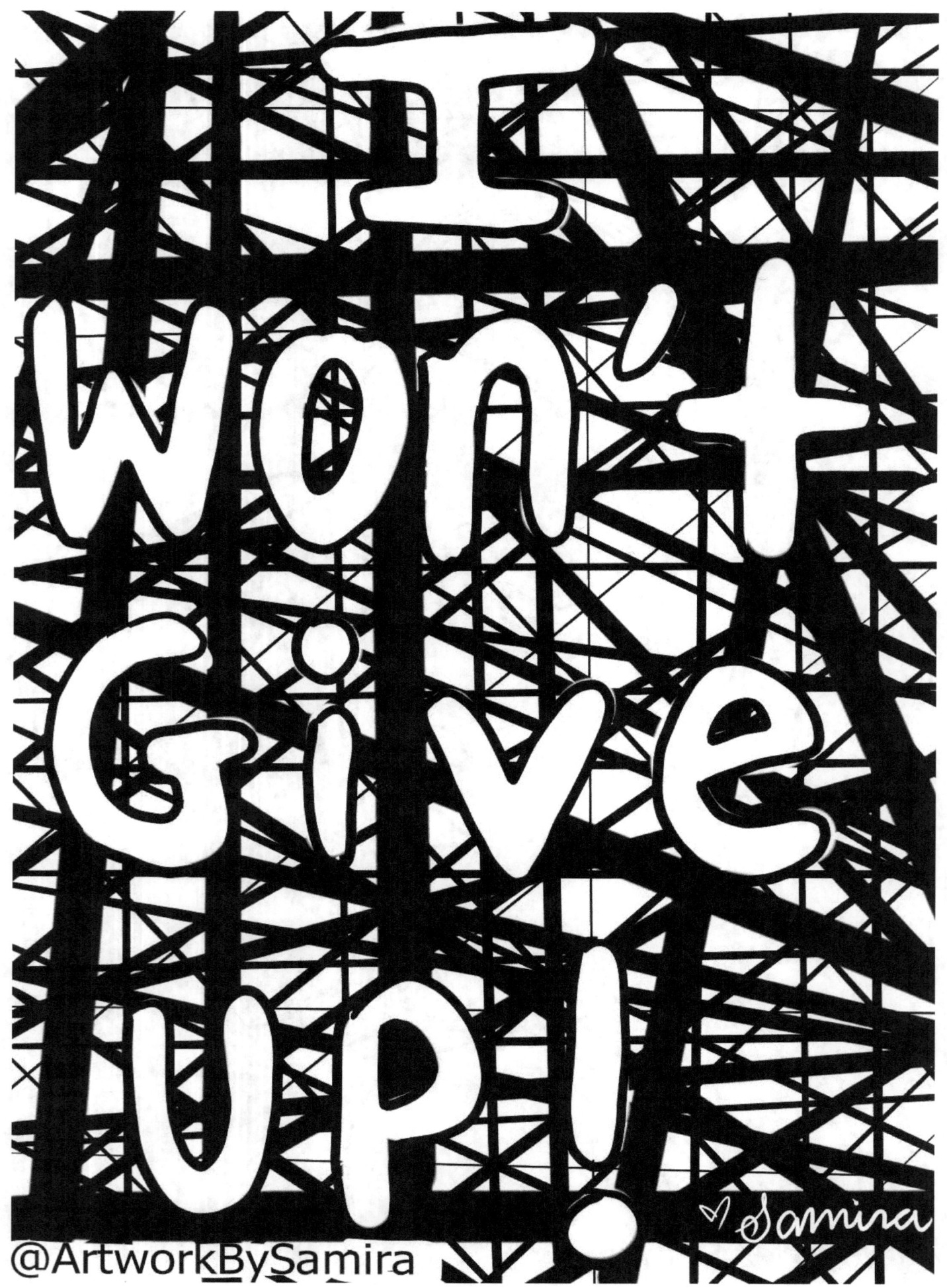

I won't Give up!

@ArtworkBySamira

♡Samira

I love the way my skin looks.

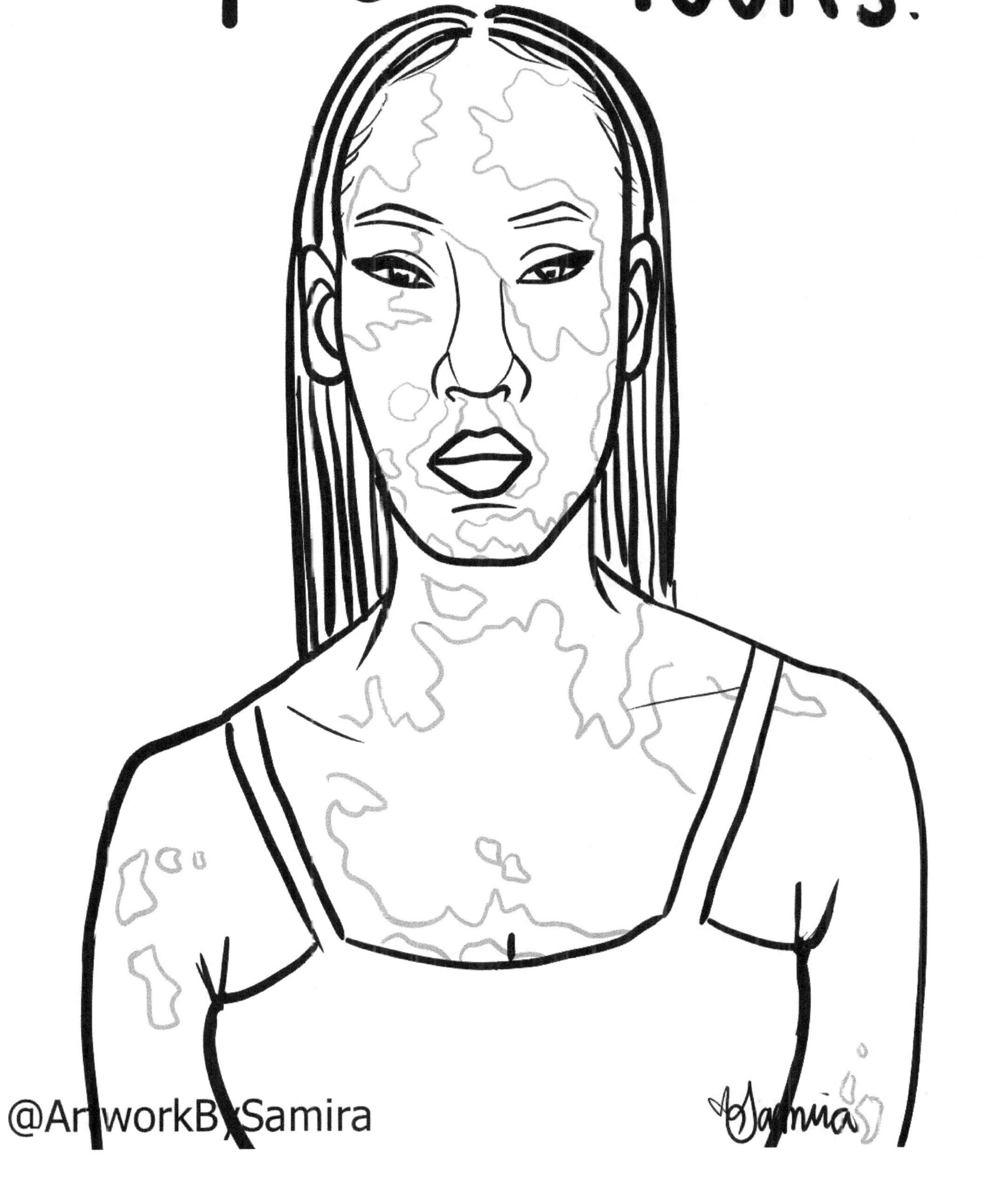

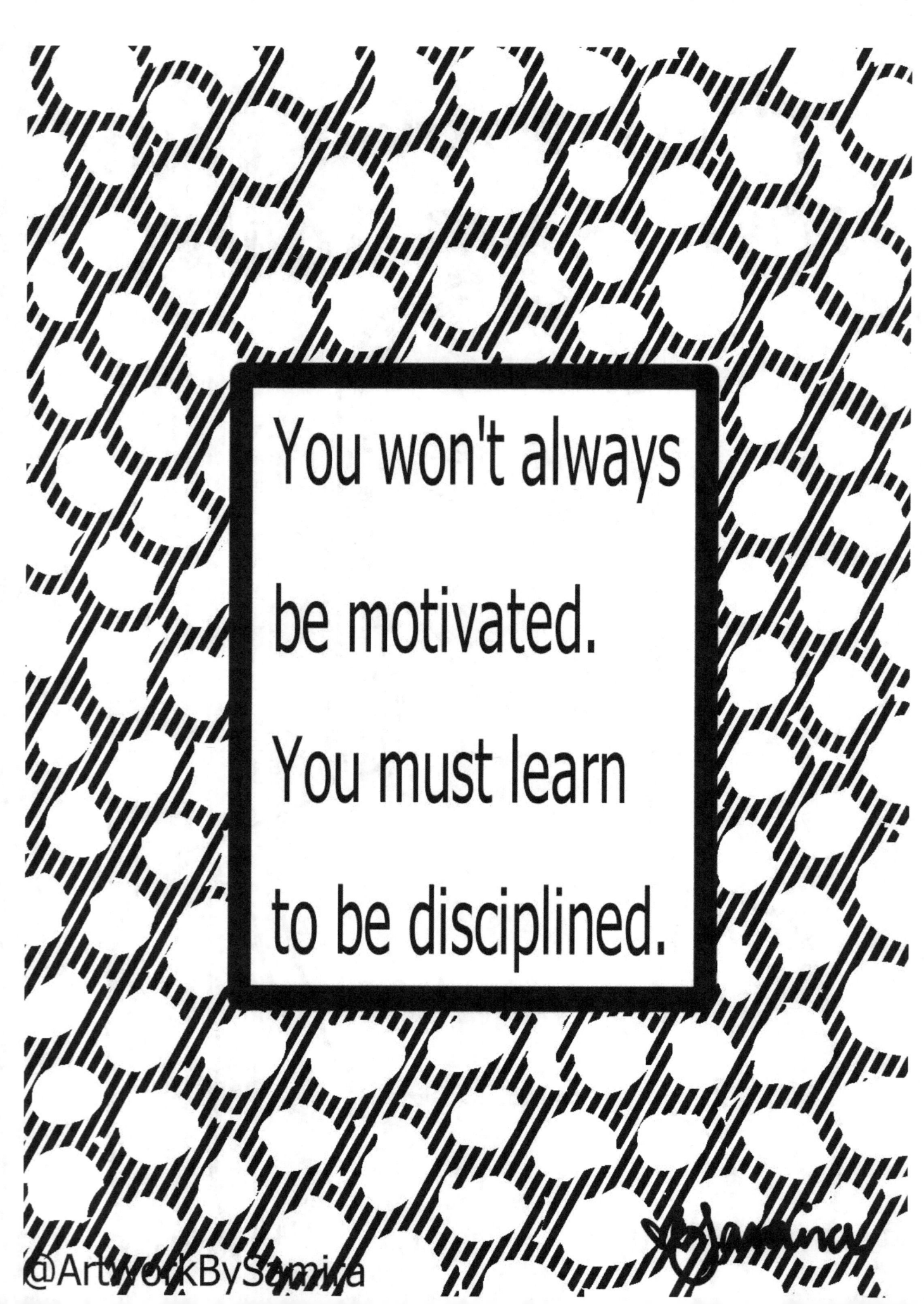

You won't always be motivated. You must learn to be disciplined.

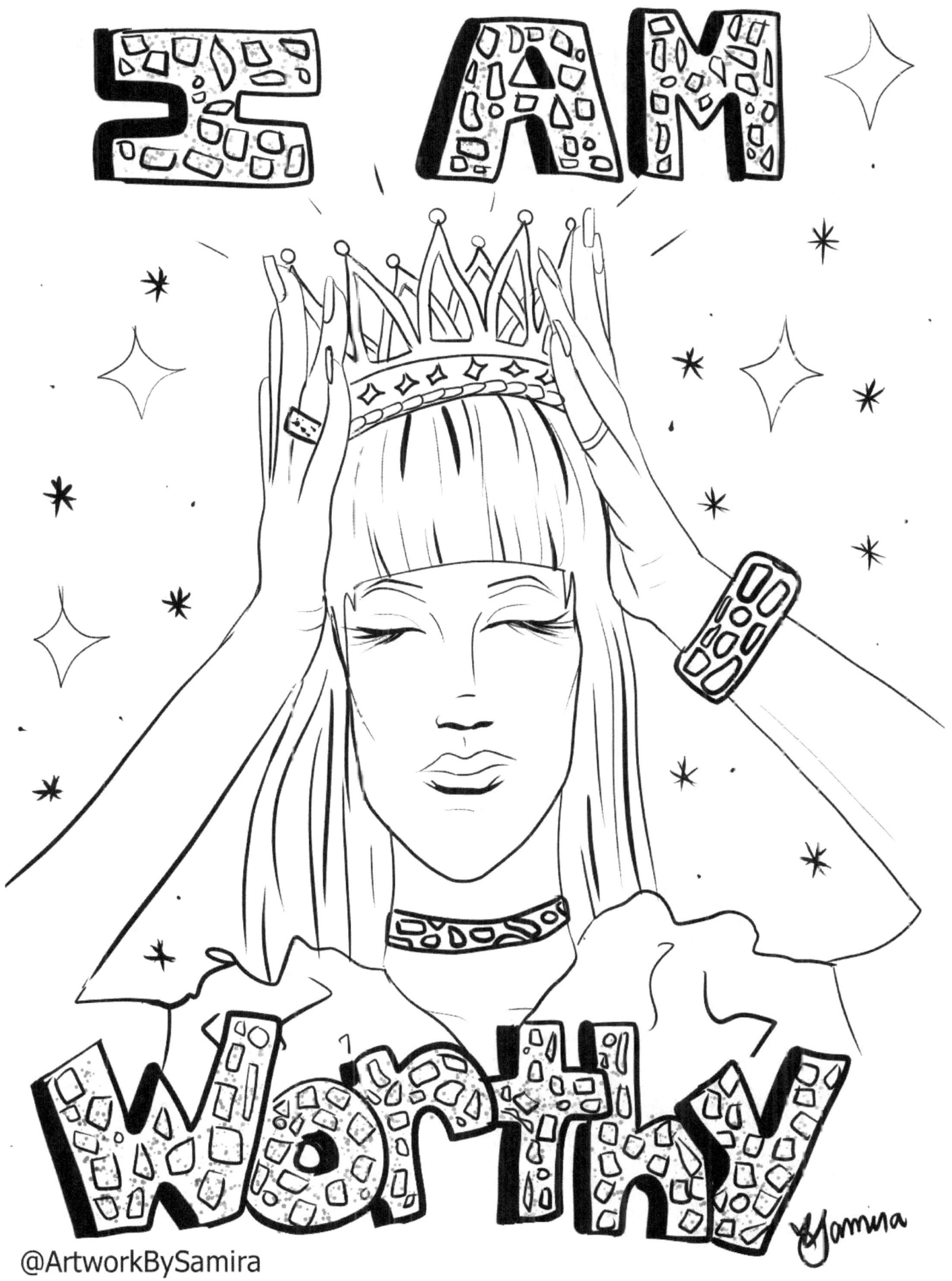

@ArtworkBySamira

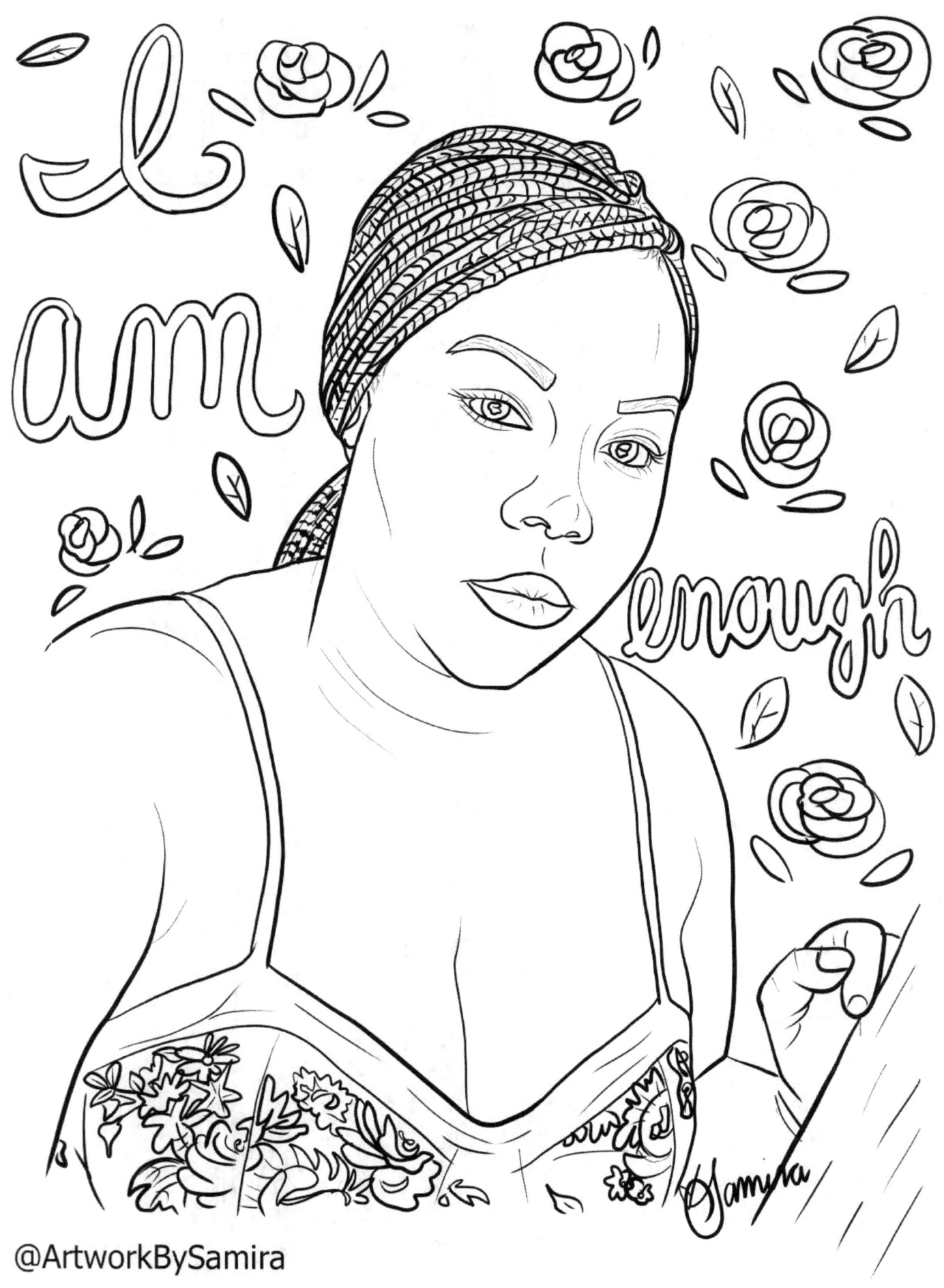

@ArtworkBySamira

Beautiful girl

YOU WERE MADE to do HARD THINGS

{So believe in yourself}

Samira

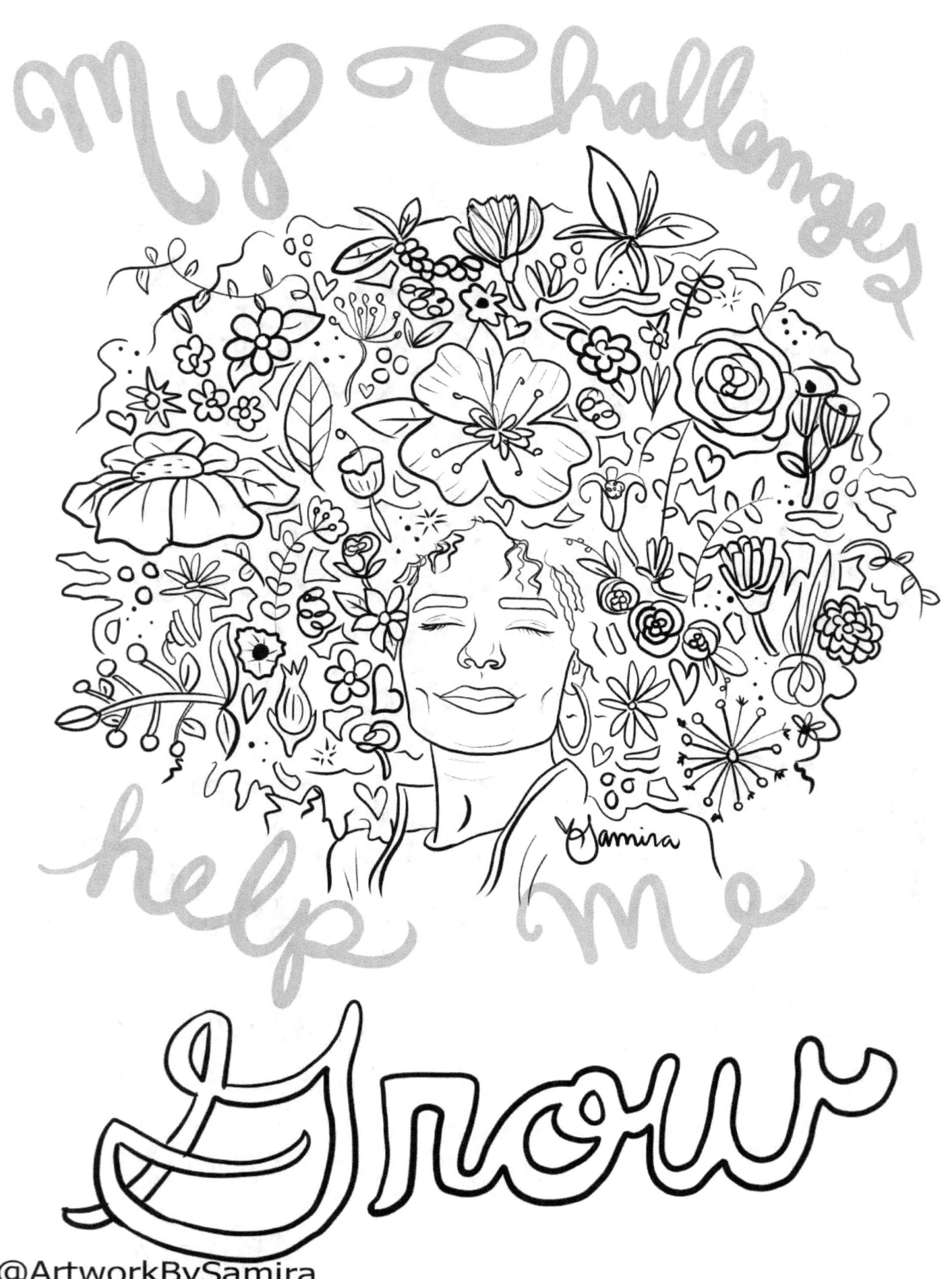

My Challenges help me Grow

@ArtworkBySamira

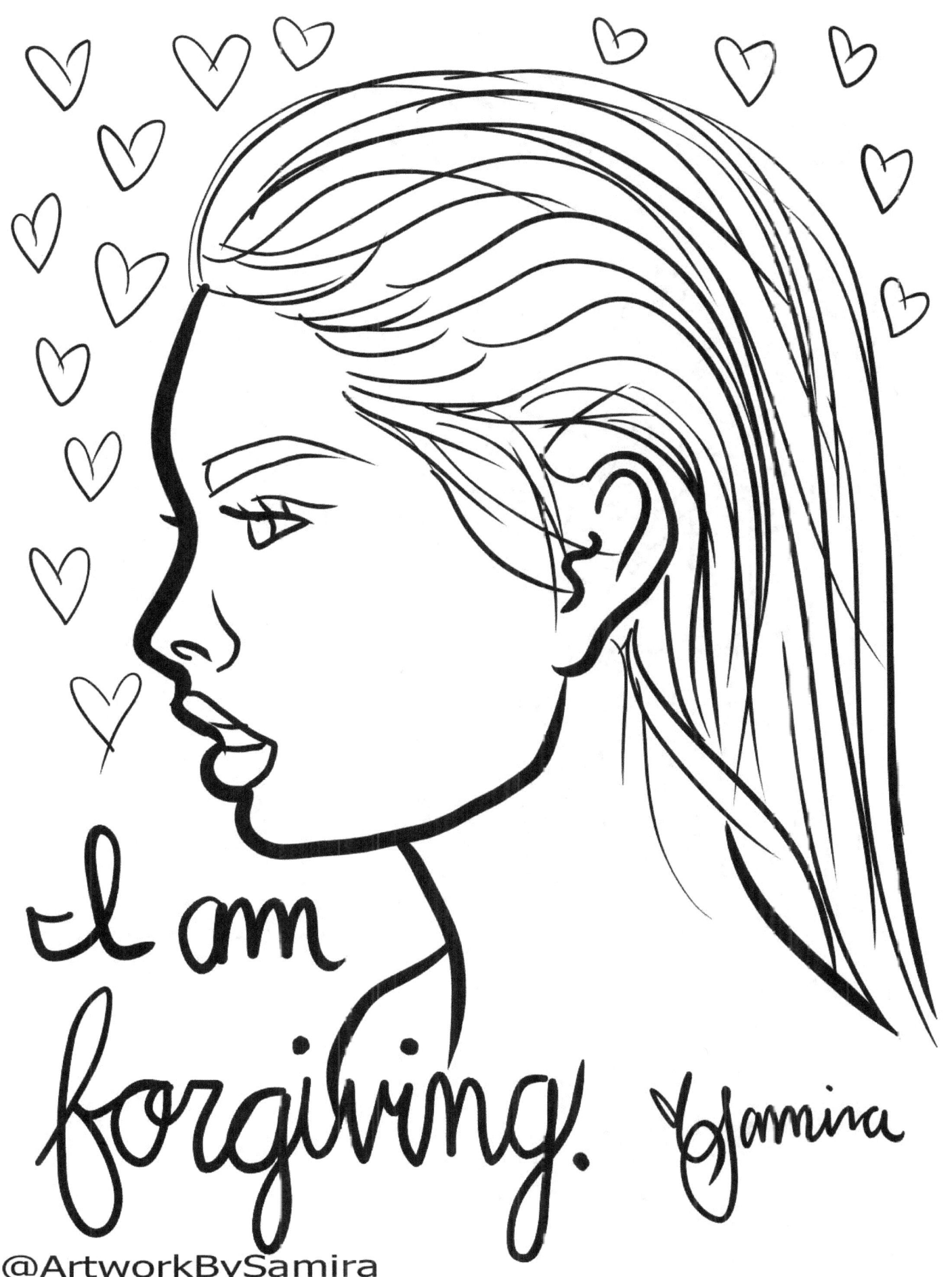

I am forgiving.

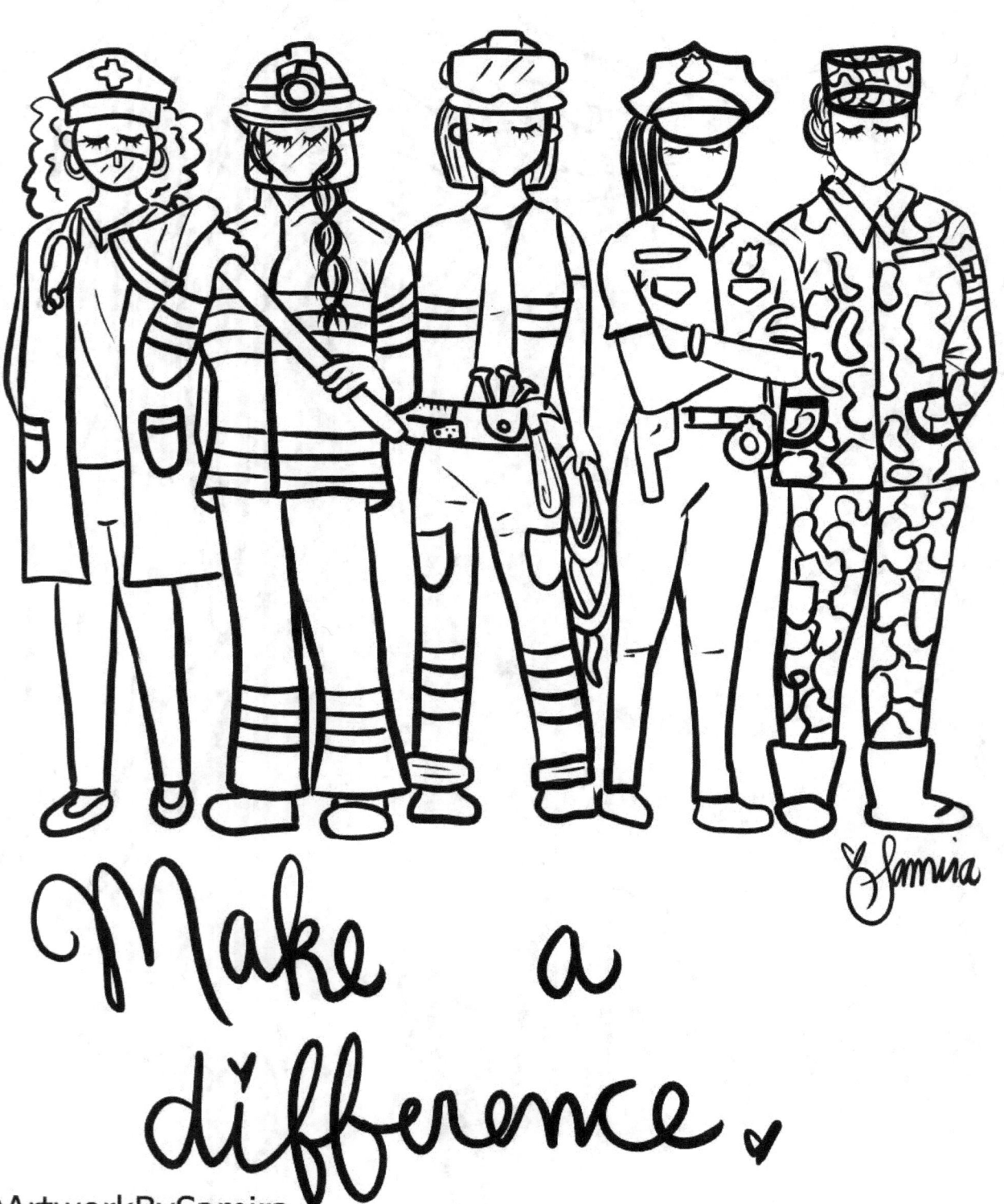

@ArtworkBySamira

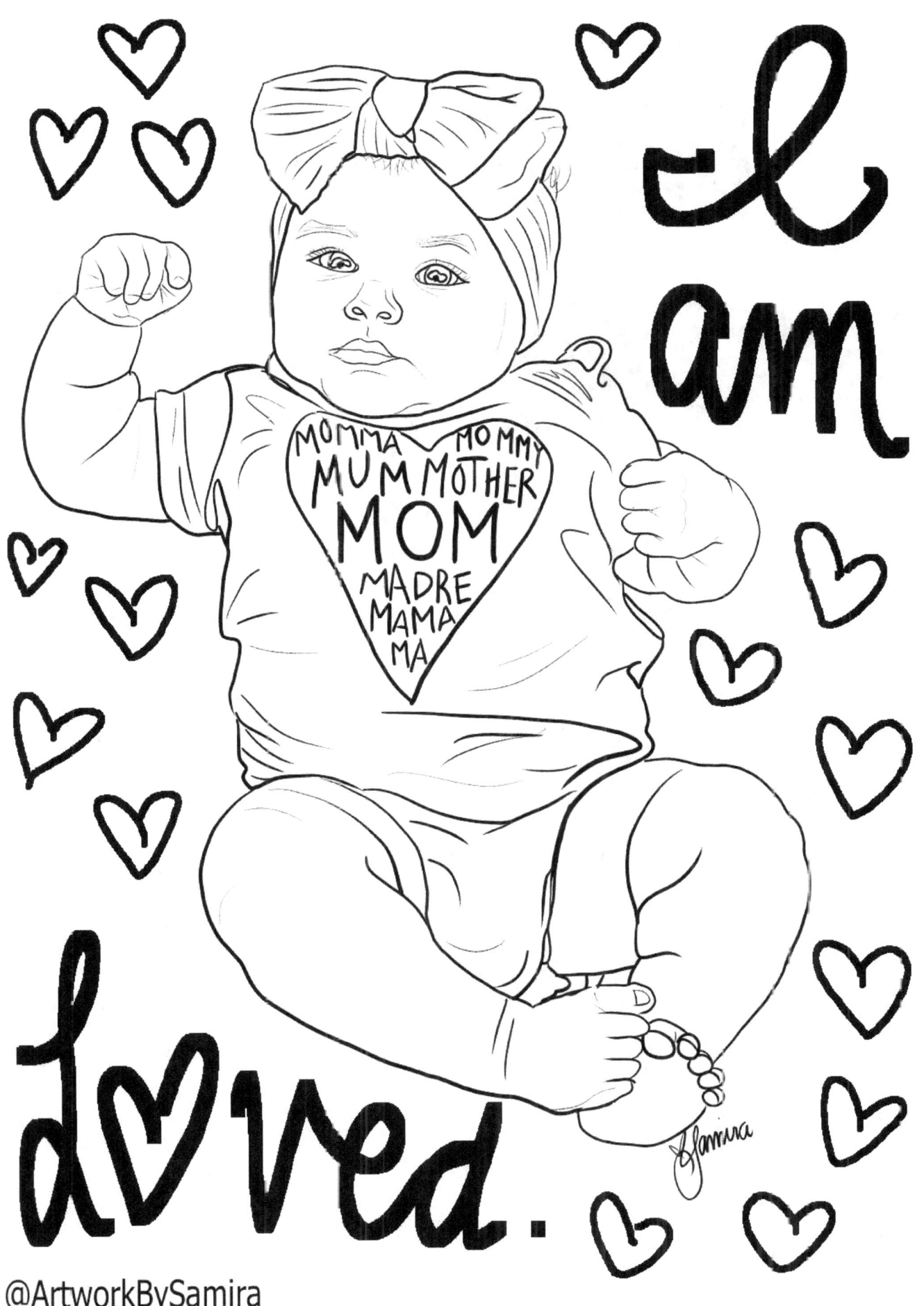

I am loved.

@ArtworkBySamira

Every day I get better

@ArtworkBySamira

≷ YOU ARE ≷

《 BRAVER 》

than you believe

《 STRONGER 》

than you seem

《 SMARTER 》

than you think

《 AND LOVED 》

More than you'll ever know

I am in charge of how I feel, and today I choose happiness.

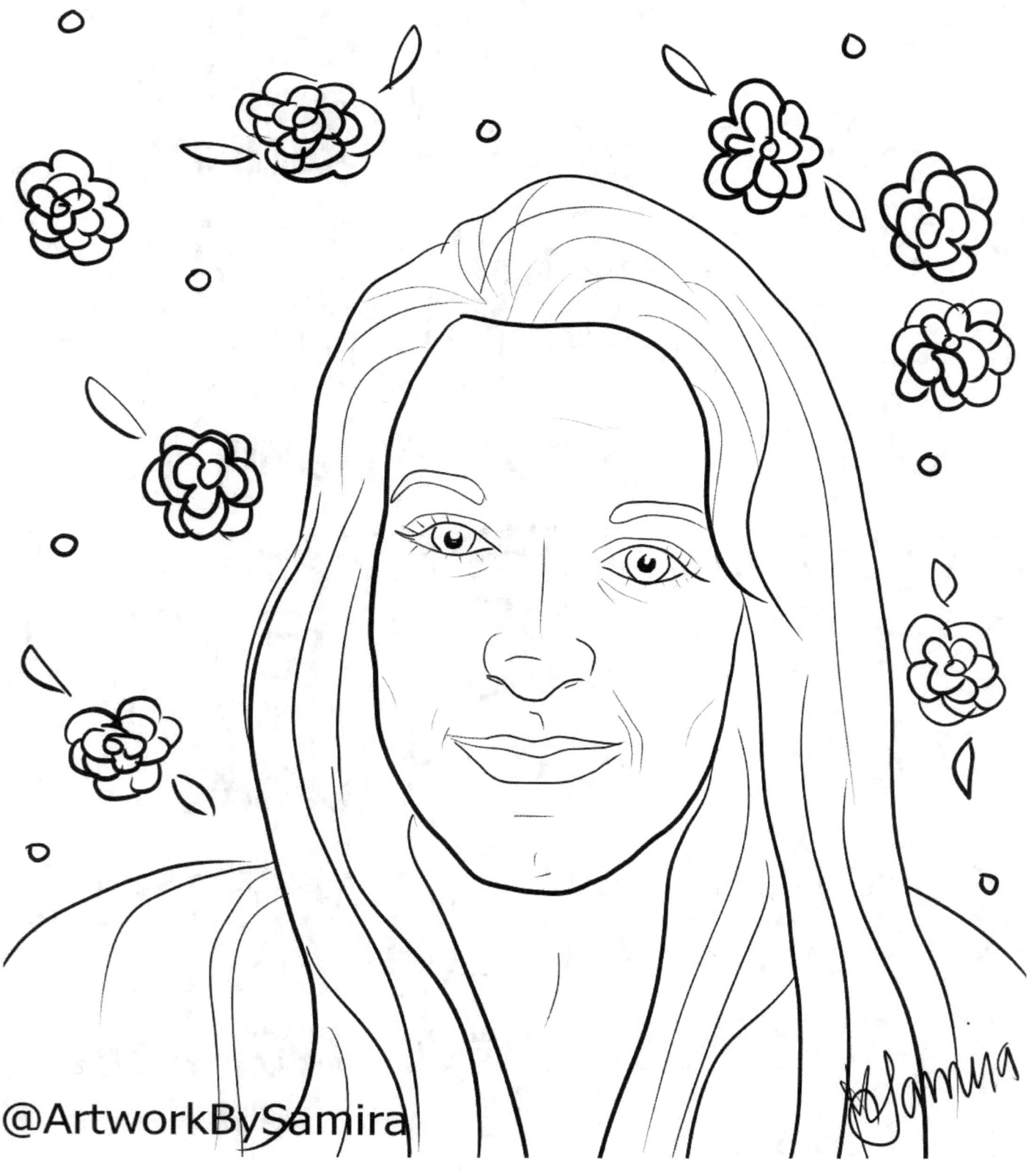

@ArtworkBySamira

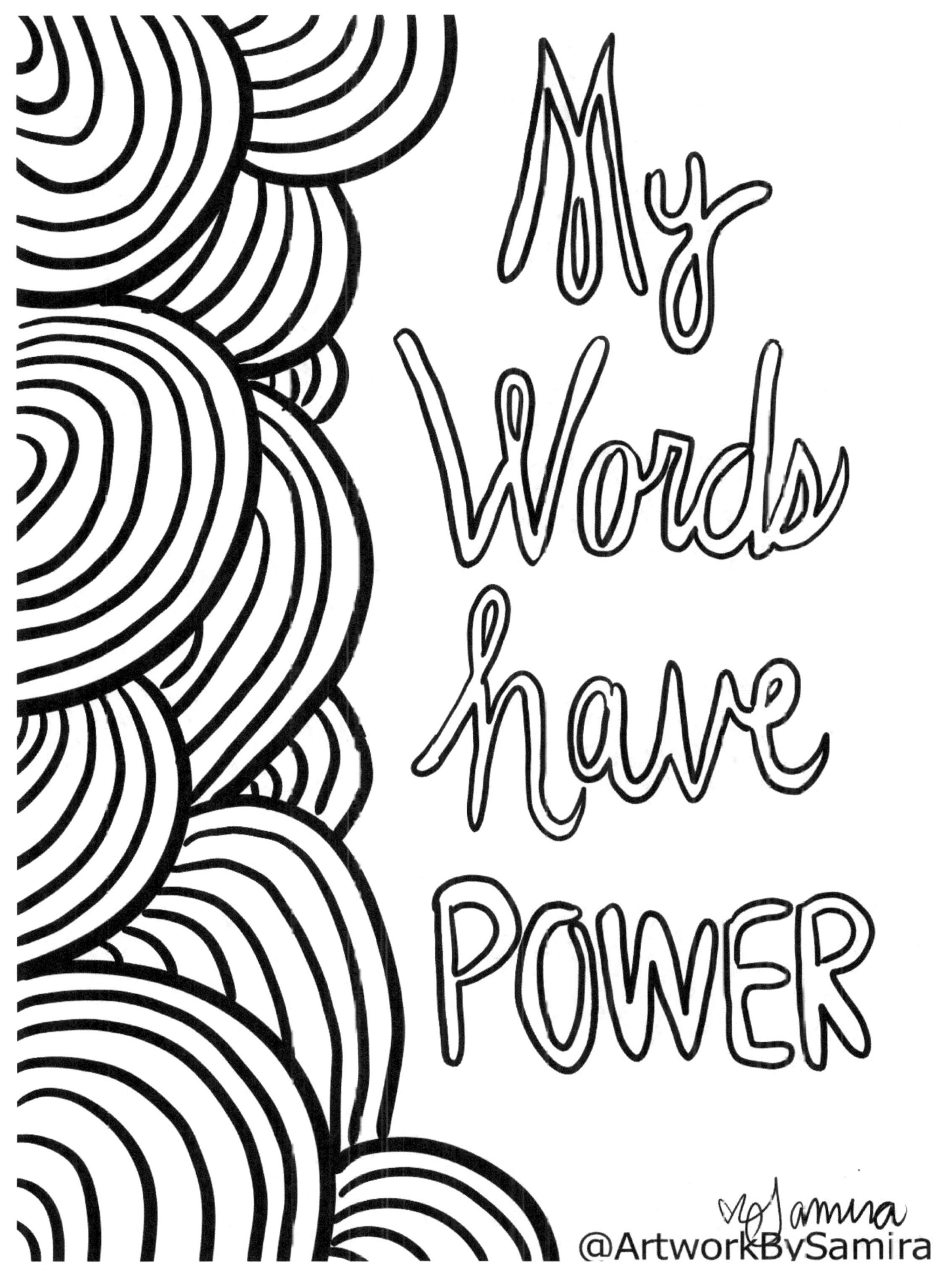

My Words have POWER

@ArtworkBySamira

I will always remember to stop, take a look around, and...

@ArtworkBySamira

Samira

Live in the MOMENT

@ArtworkBySamira

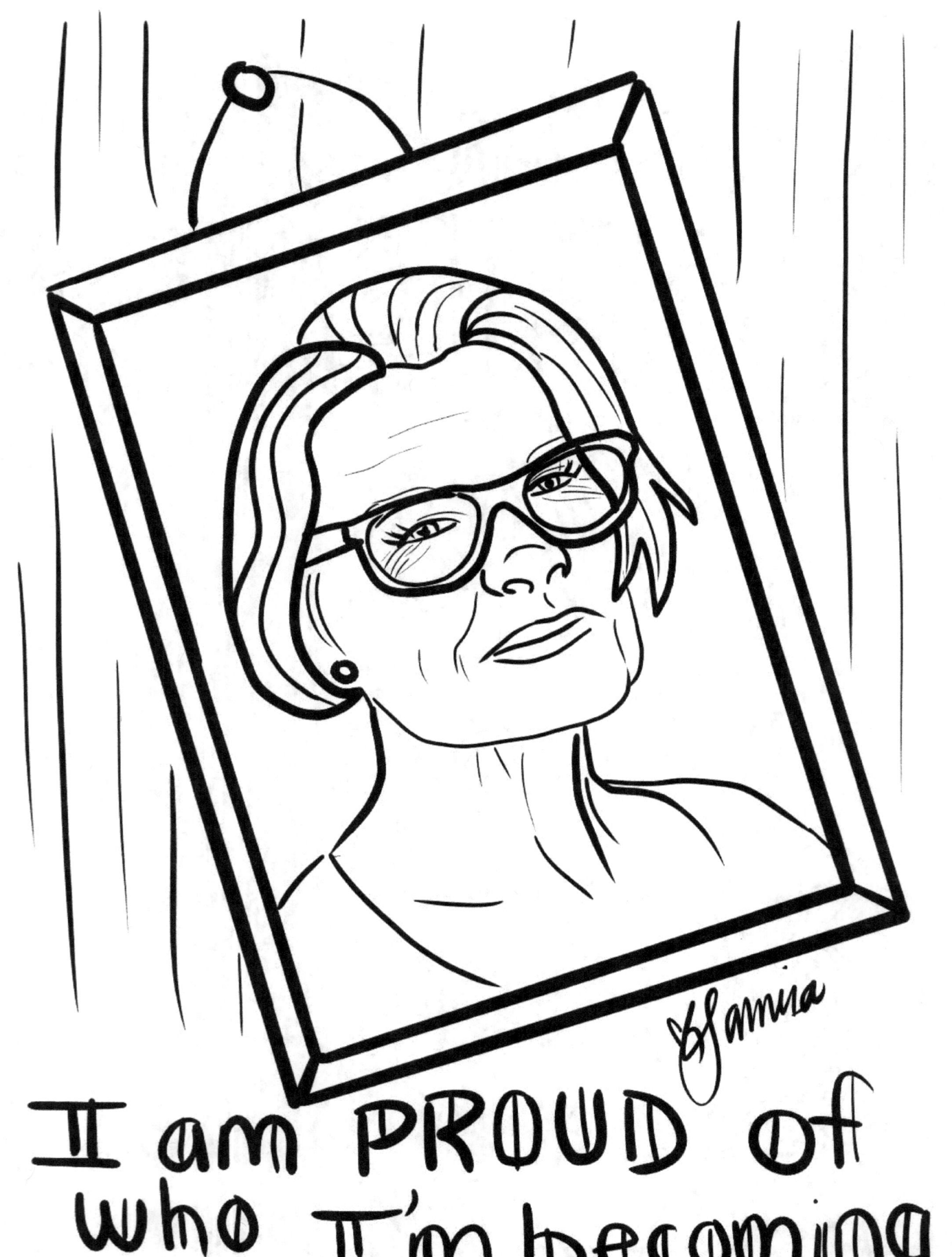

I am PROUD of who I'm becoming.

@ArtworkBySamira

Today I Start L♥ving Myself more ♥

@ArtworkBySamira

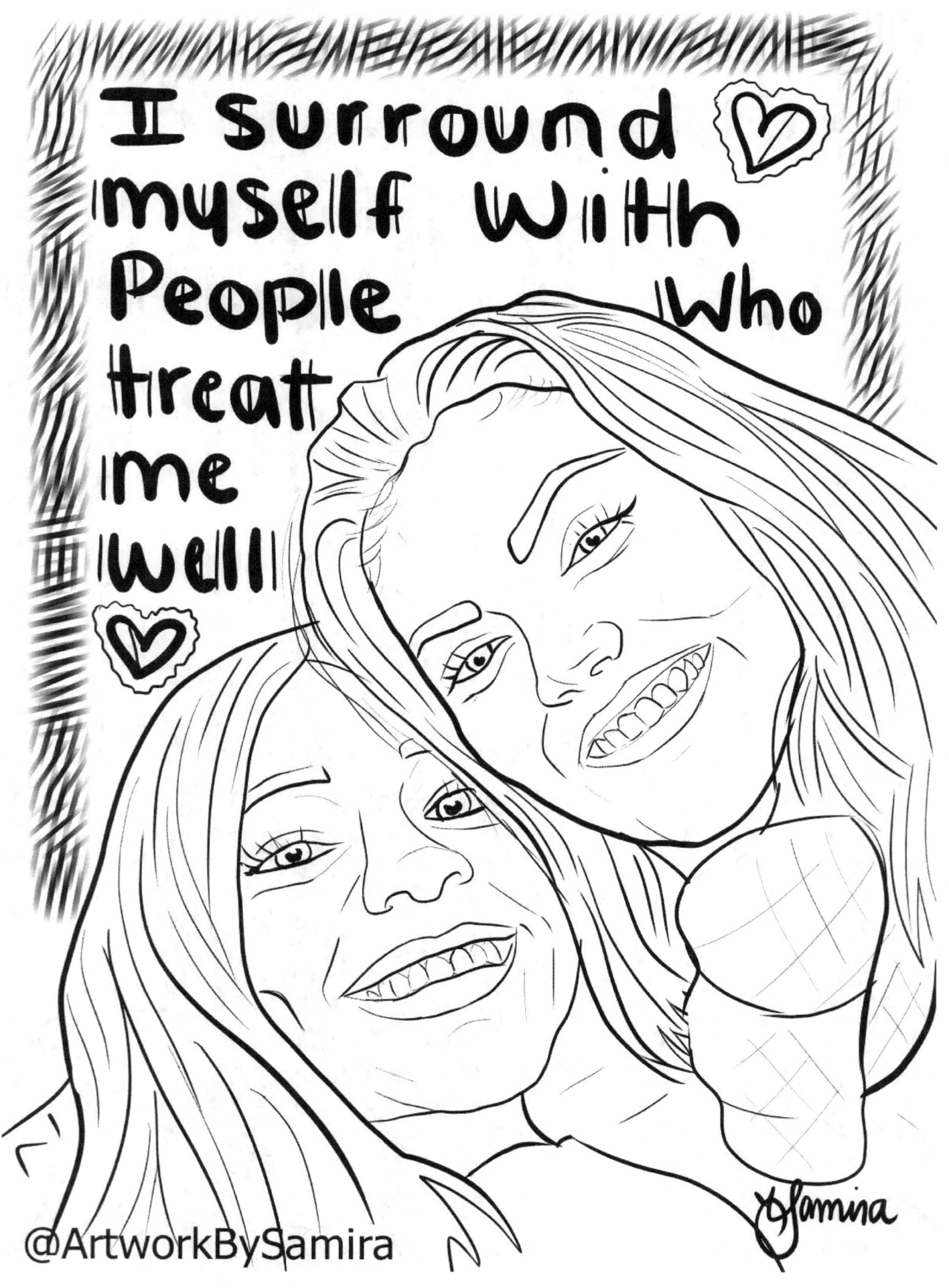

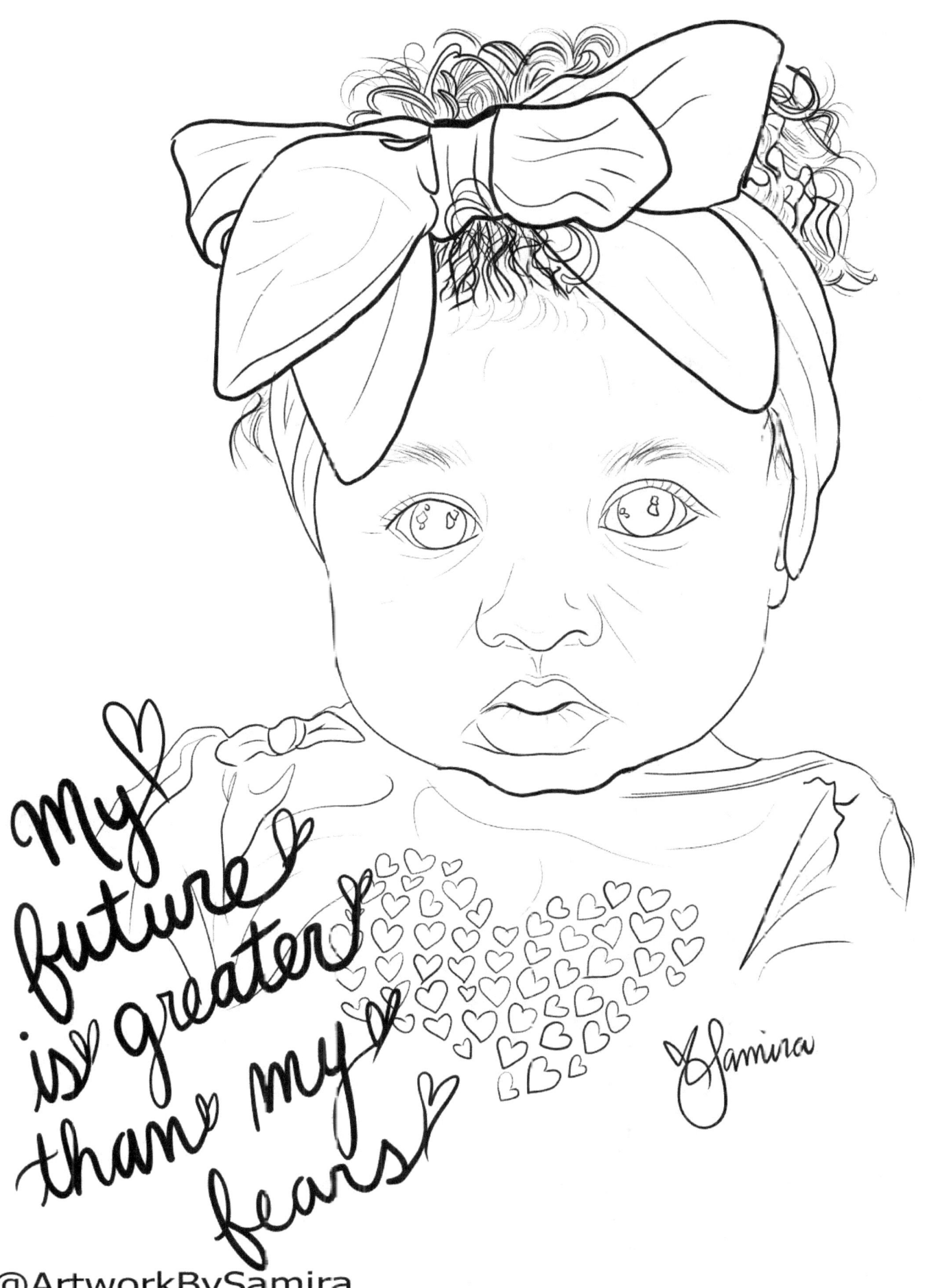

My future is greater than my fears

@ArtworkBySamira

I will not be another flower, picked for my beauty and left to die. I will be wild, difficult to find, and impossible to forget. -Erin Van Vuren

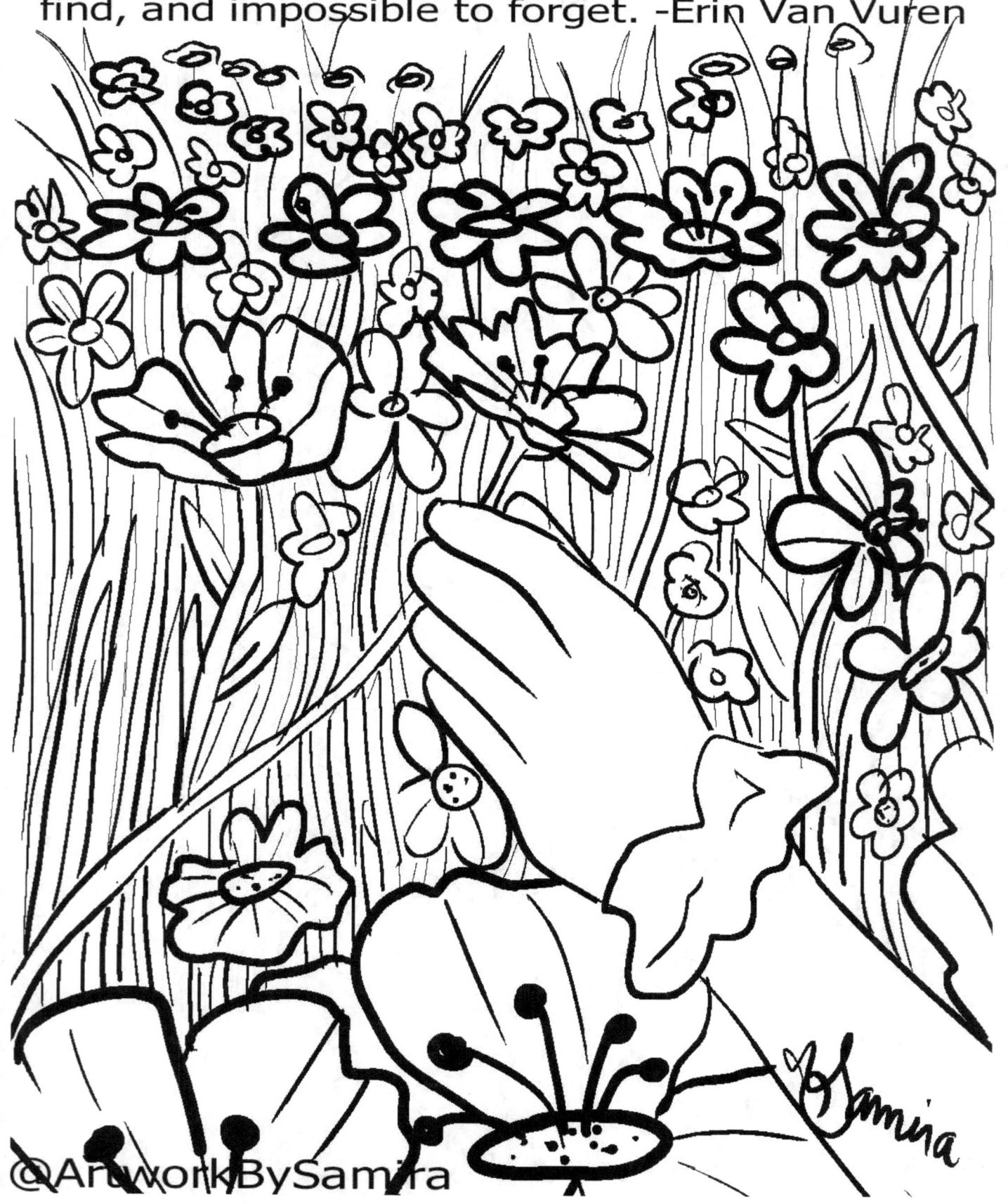

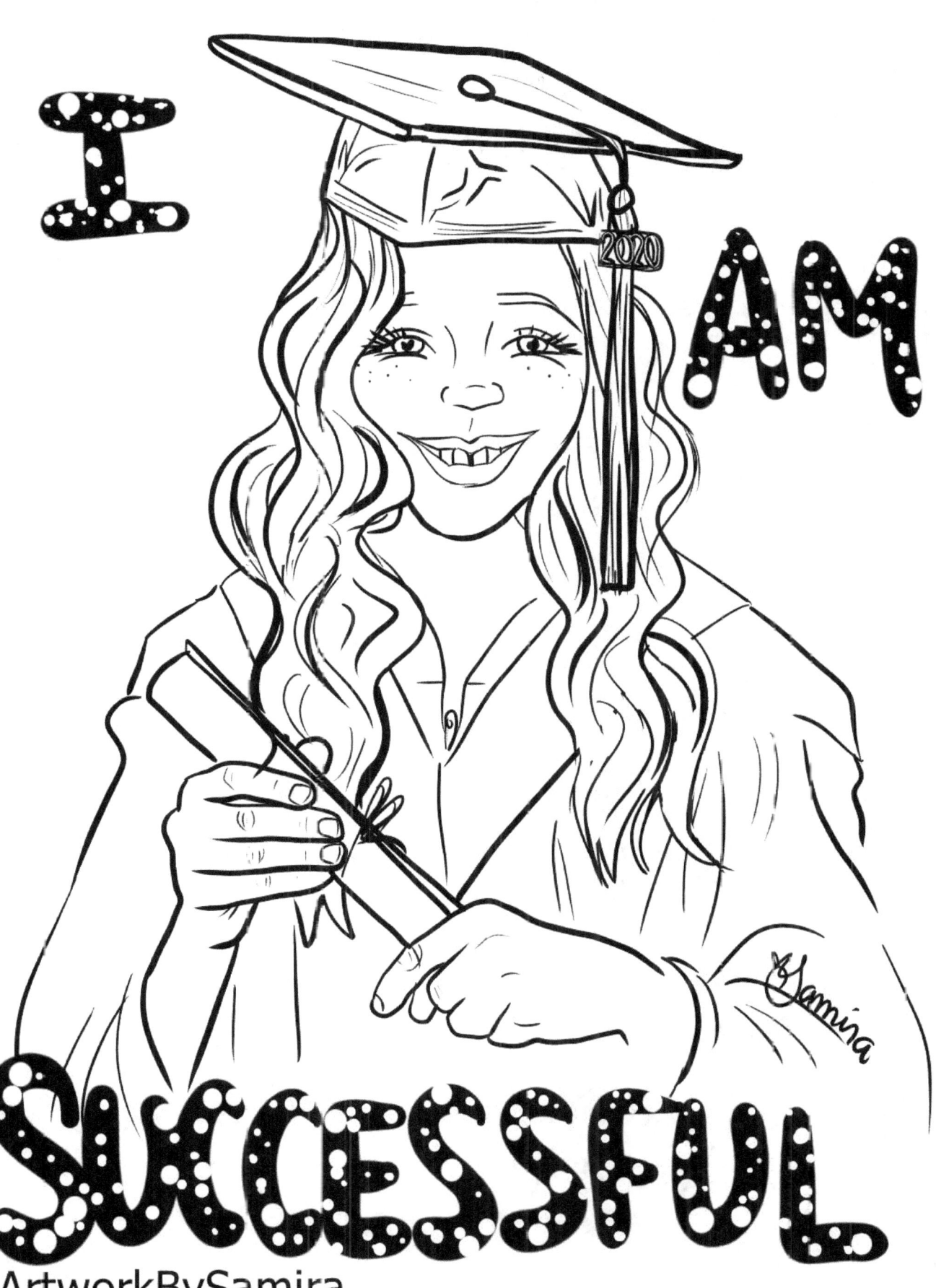

I AM SUCCESSFUL

@ArtworkBySamira

By helping others, I remind myself that I am blessed.♡

@ArtworkBySamira

Samira

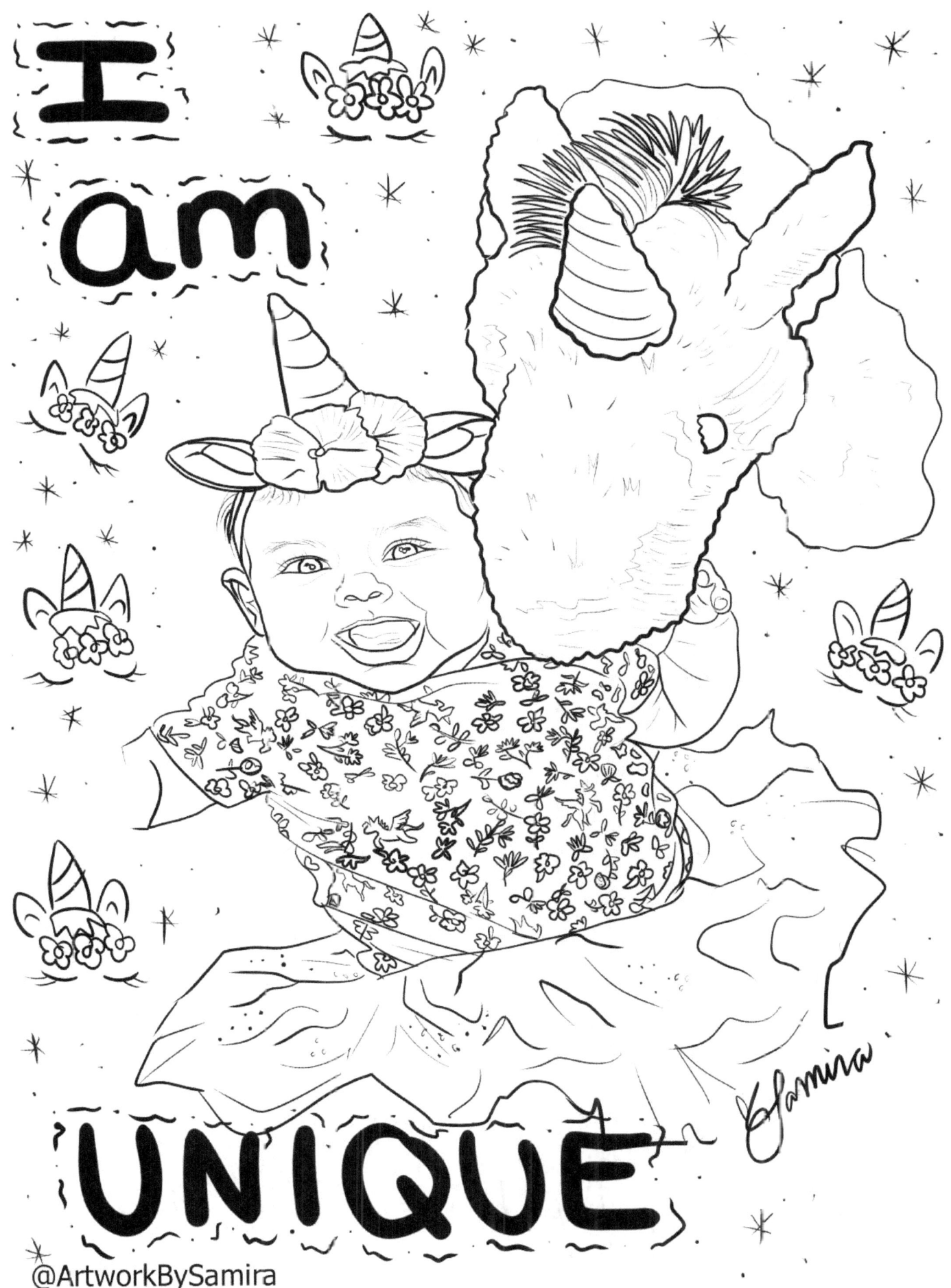

I am UNIQUE

@ArtworkBySamira

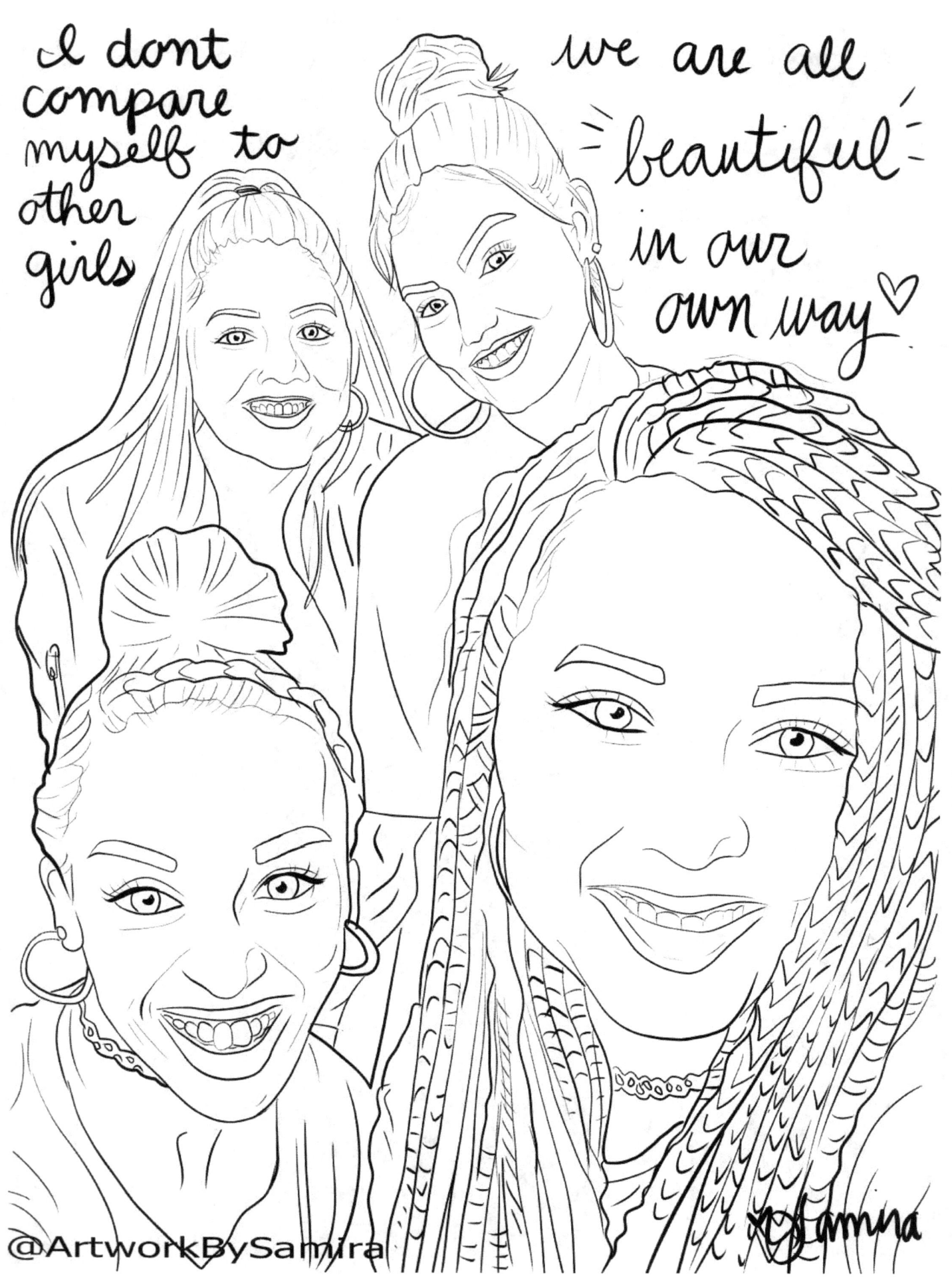

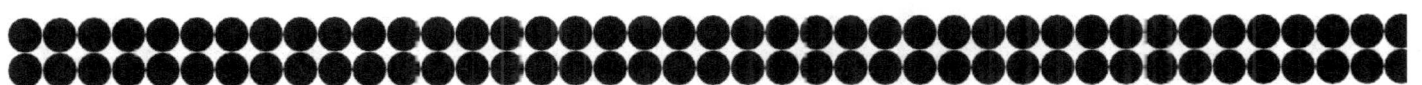
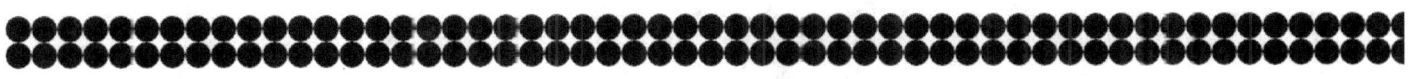

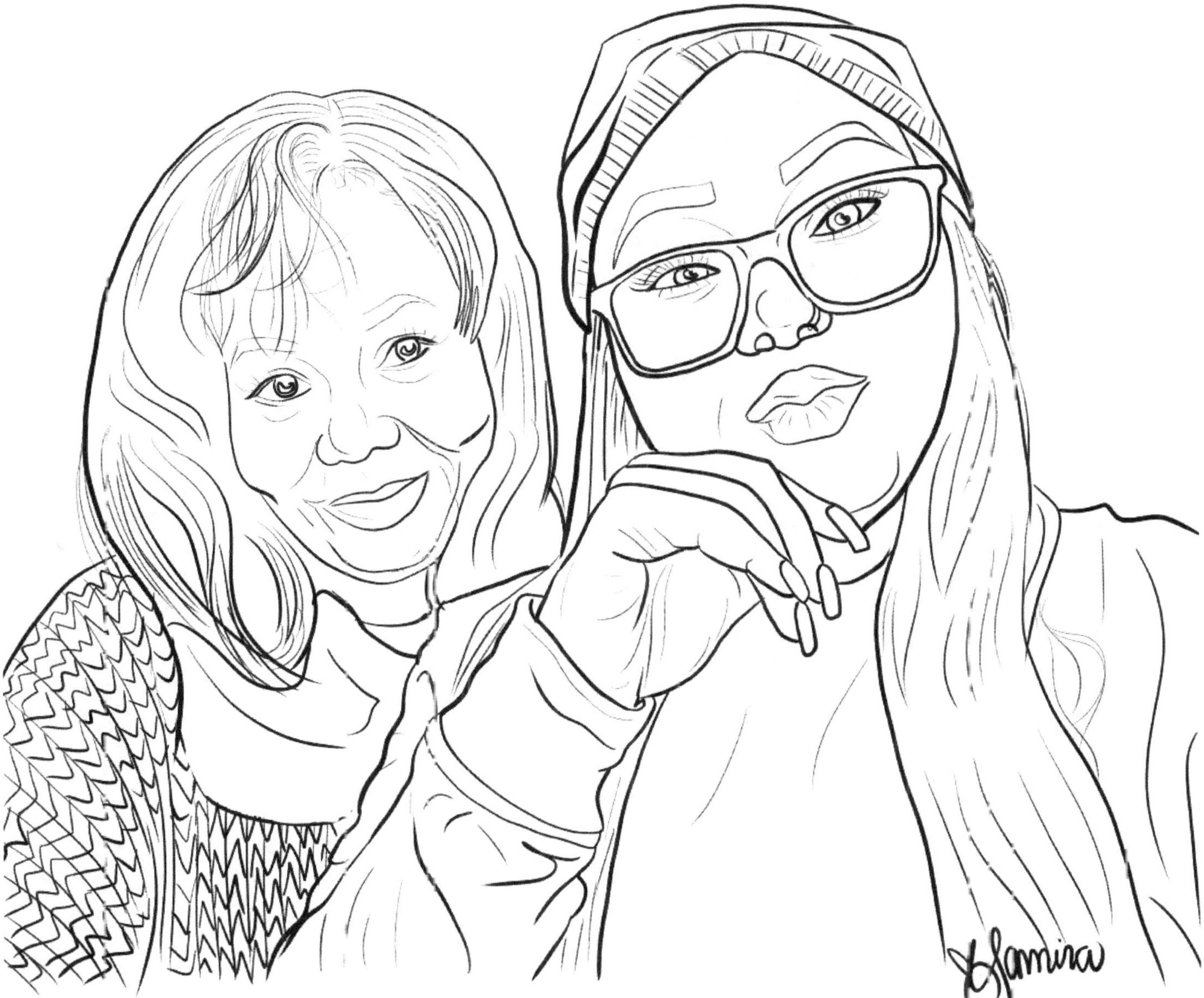

@ArtworkBySamira

WE HAVE THE POWER
TO CREATE CHANGE

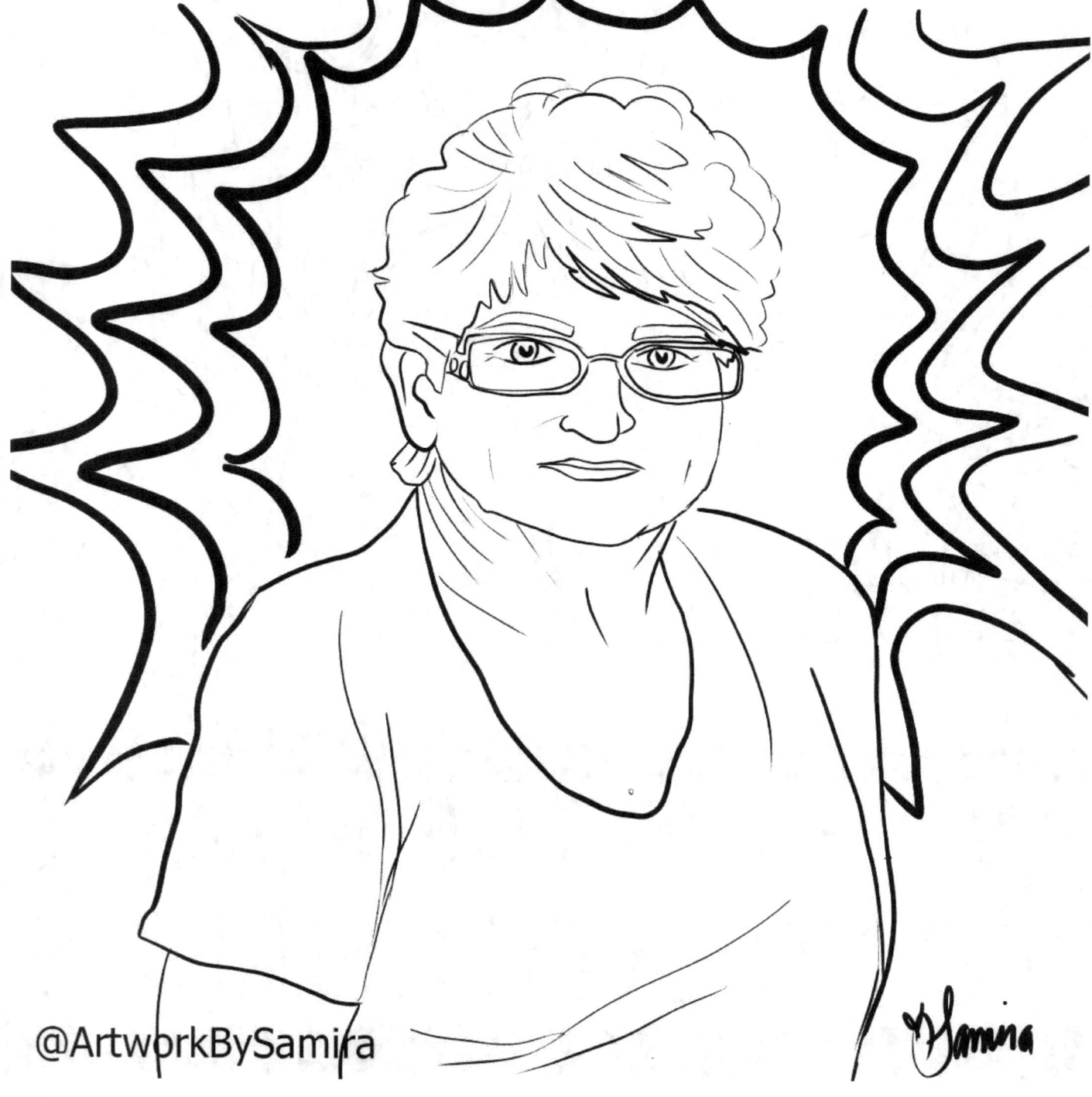

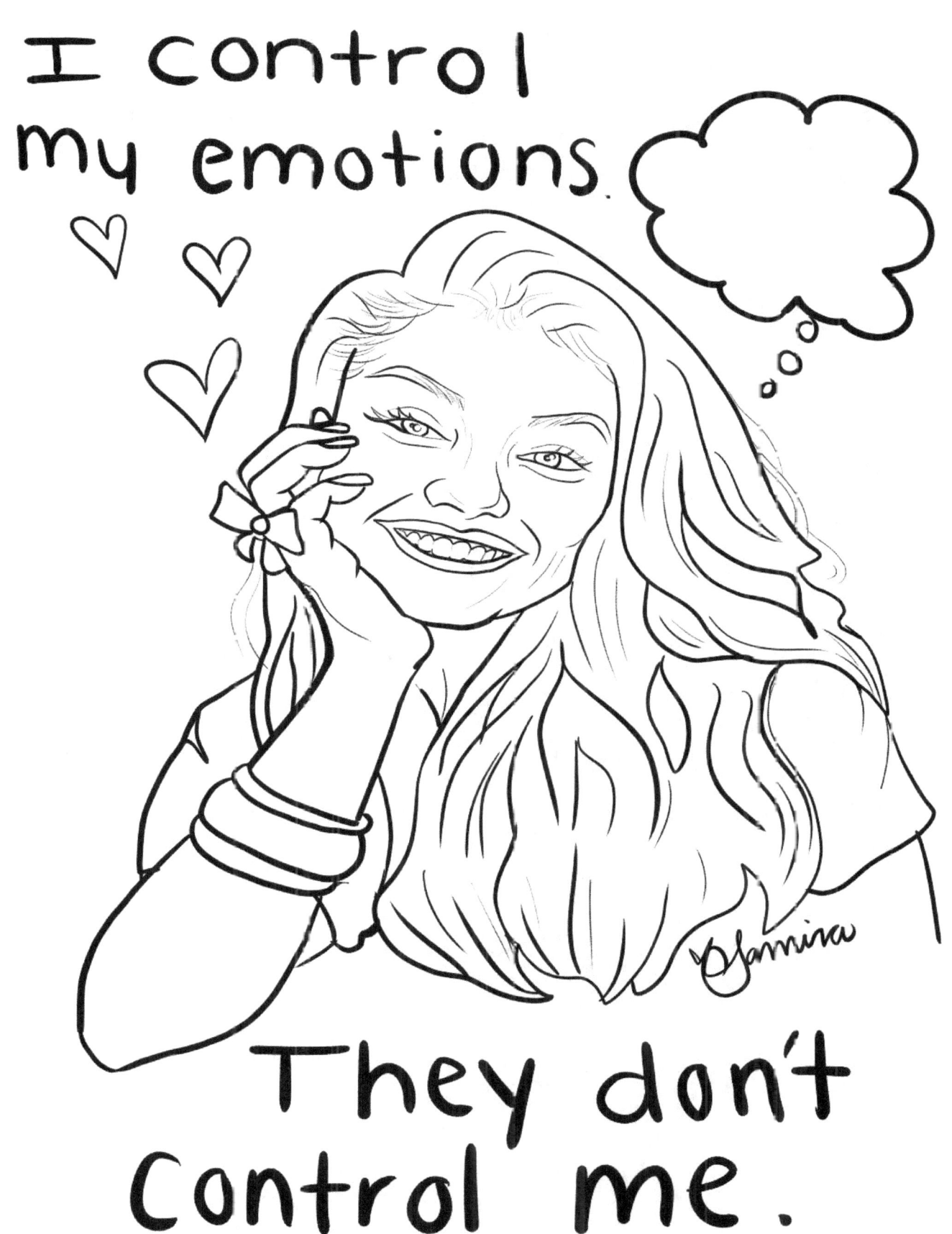

@ArtworkBySamira

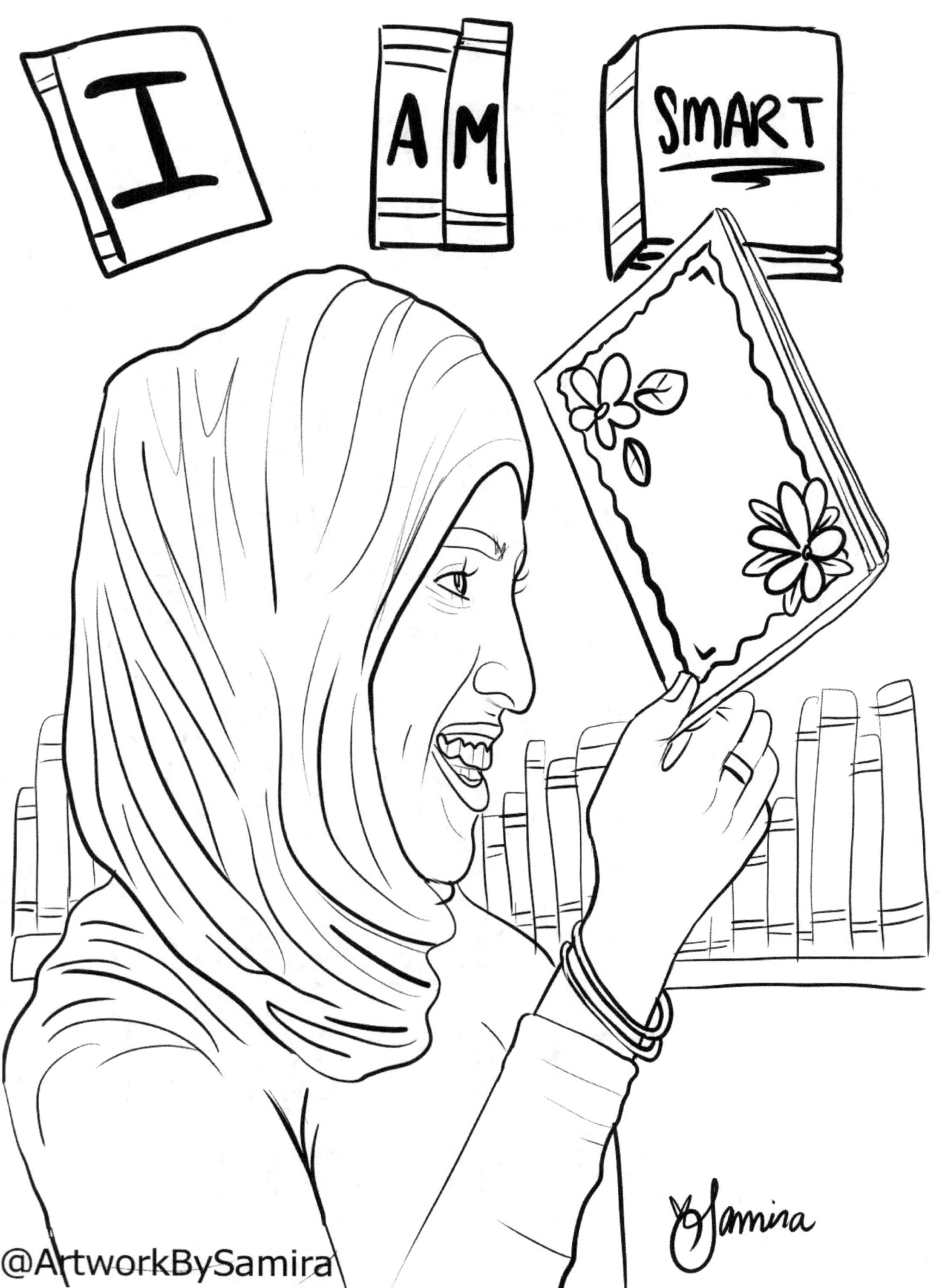

@ArtworkBySamira

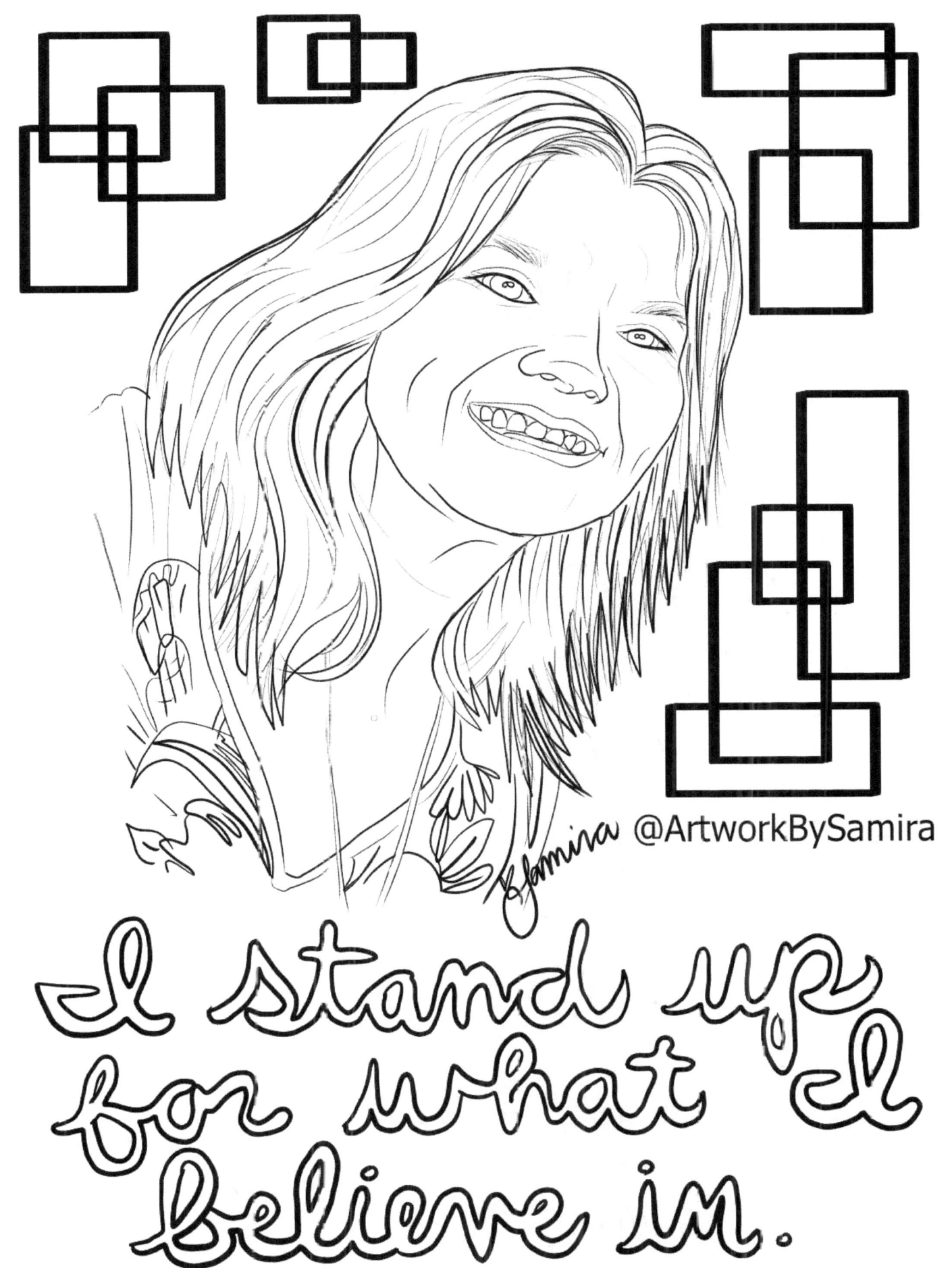

@ArtworkBySamira

I stand up for what I believe in.

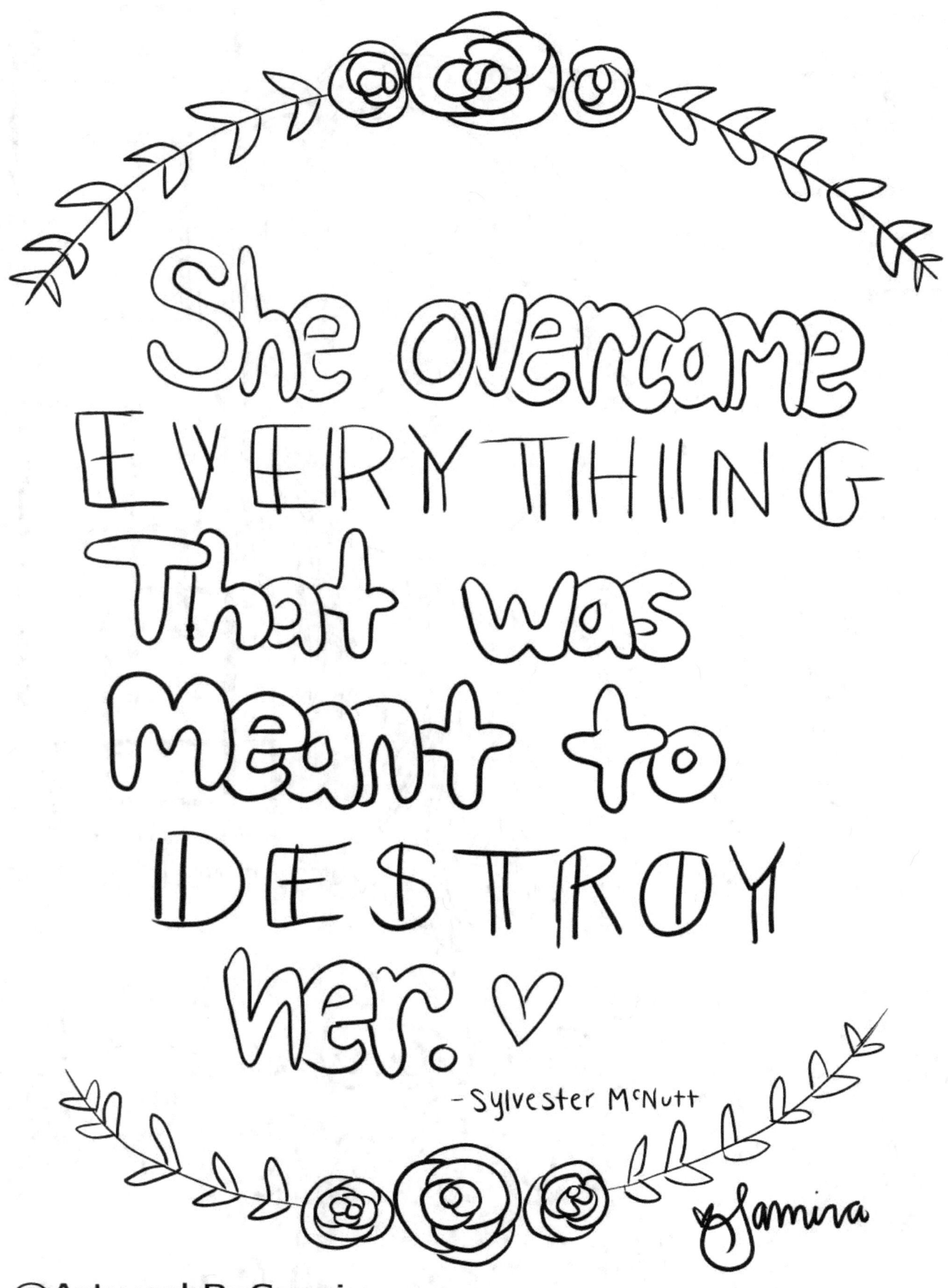

She overcame EVERYTHING That was Meant to DESTROY her. ♡

-Sylvester McNutt

@ArtworkBySamira

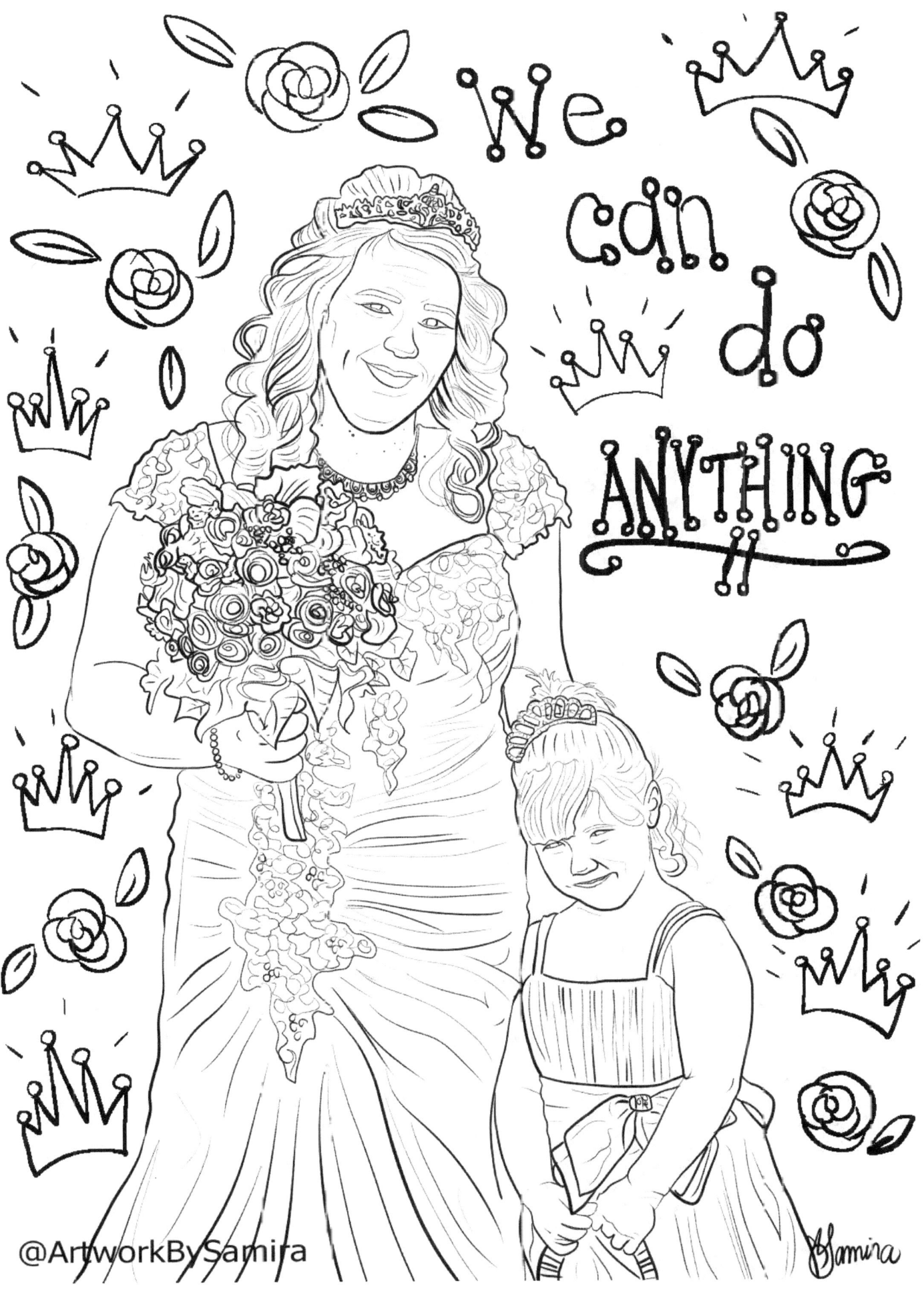

We can do ANYTHING!!

@ArtworkBySamira

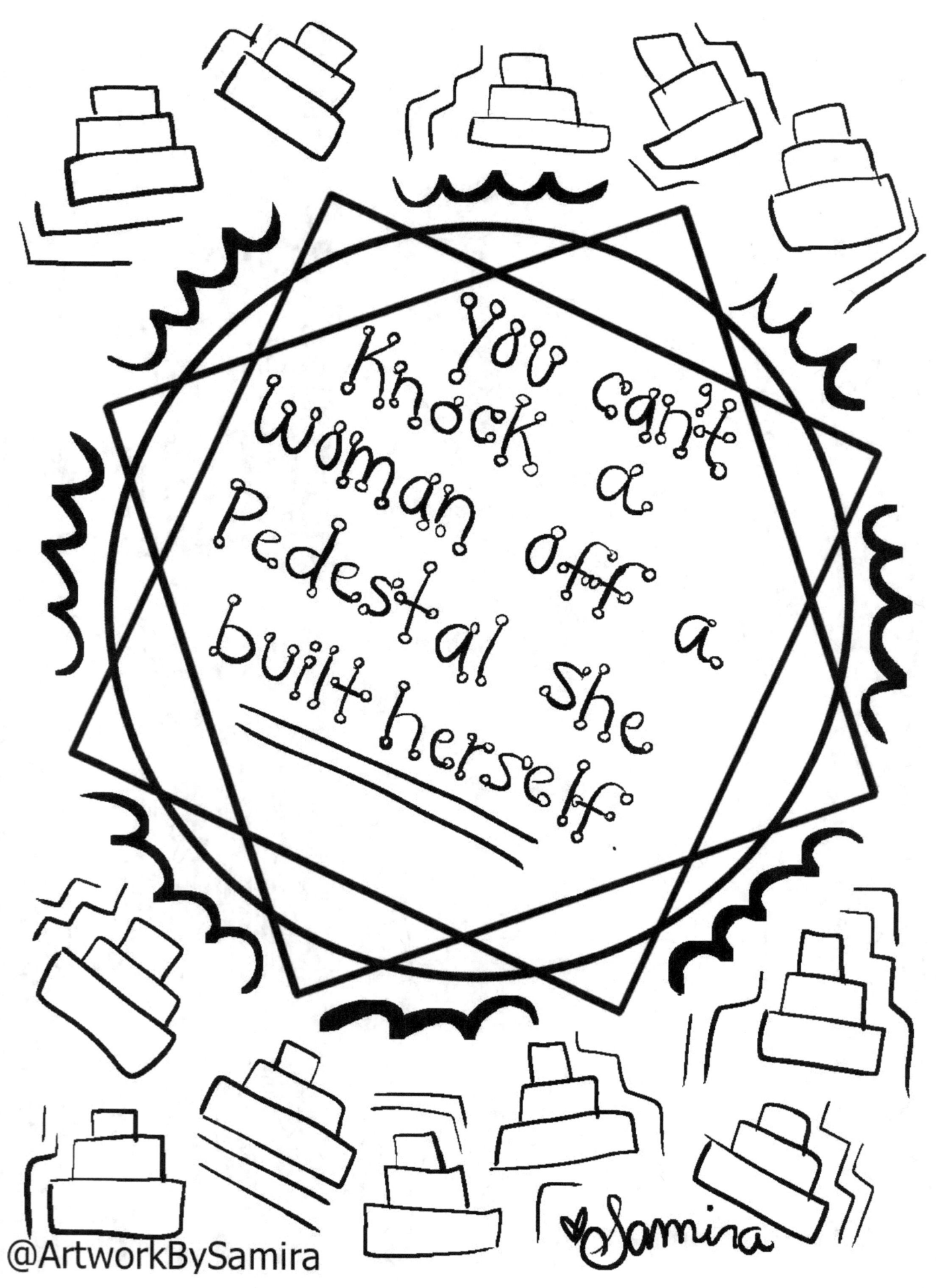

You can't knock a woman off a pedestal she built herself.

My hair is PERFECT
The way it is

@ArtworkBySamira

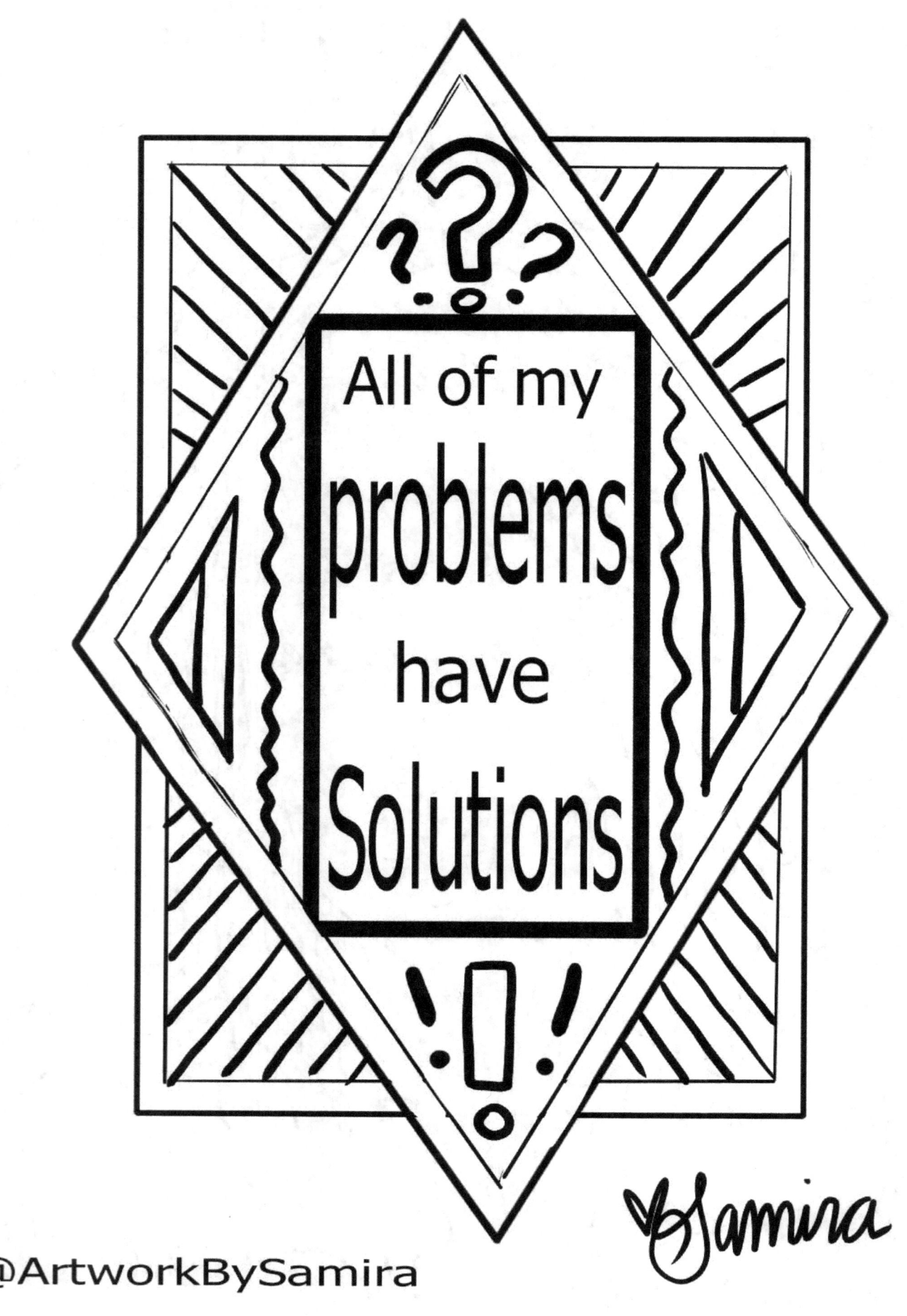

All of my problems have Solutions

@ArtworkBySamira

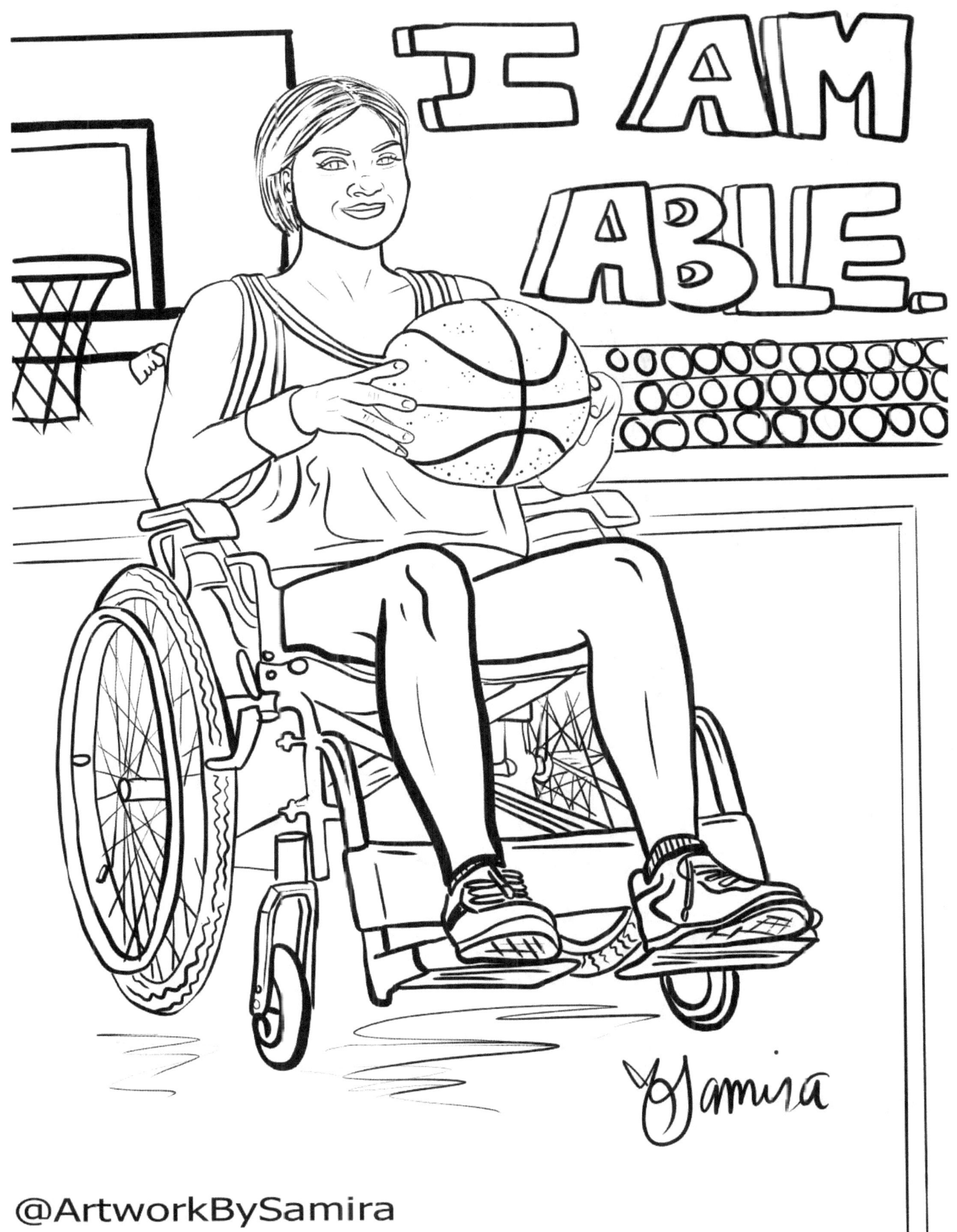

@ArtworkBySamira

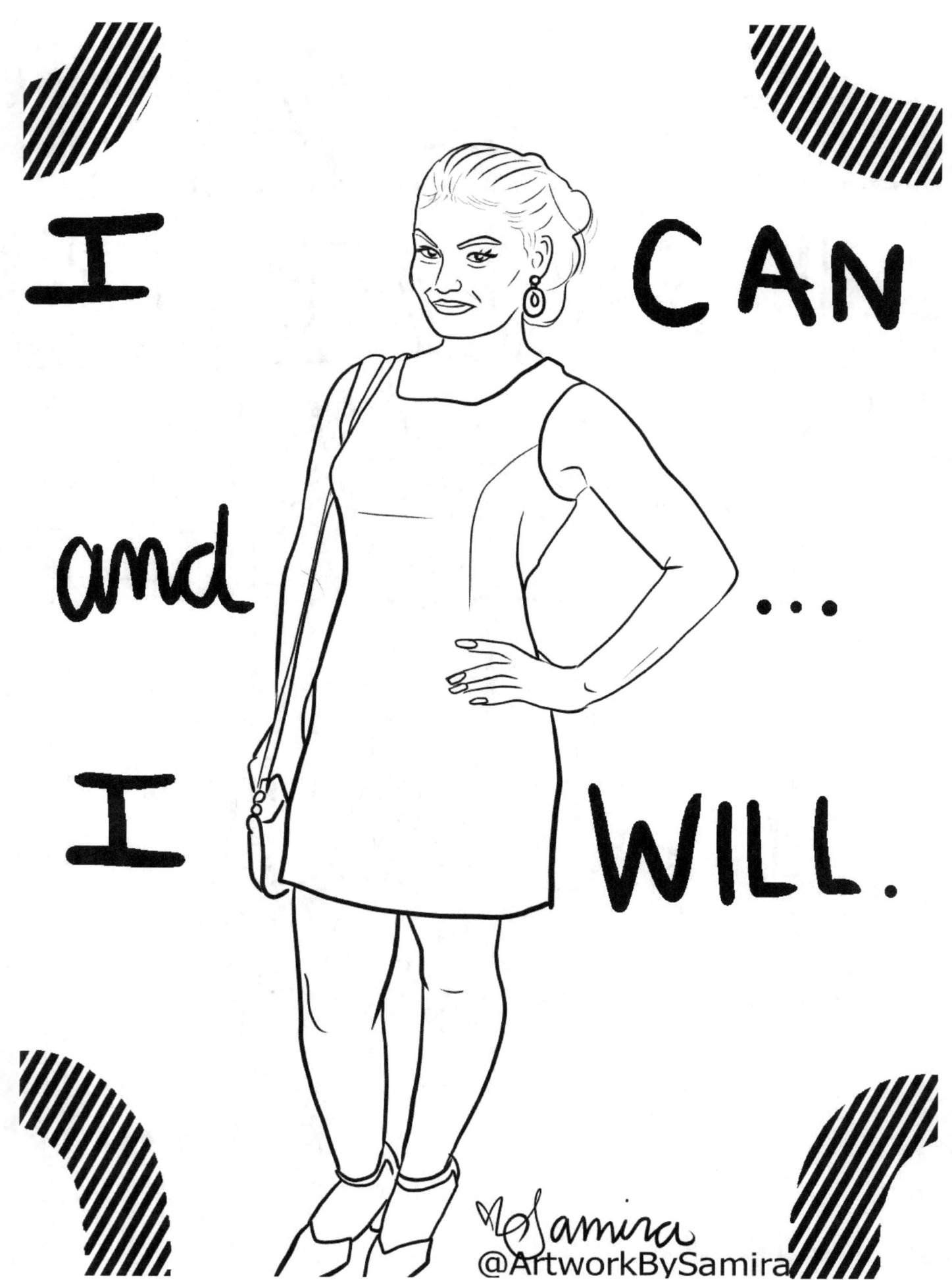

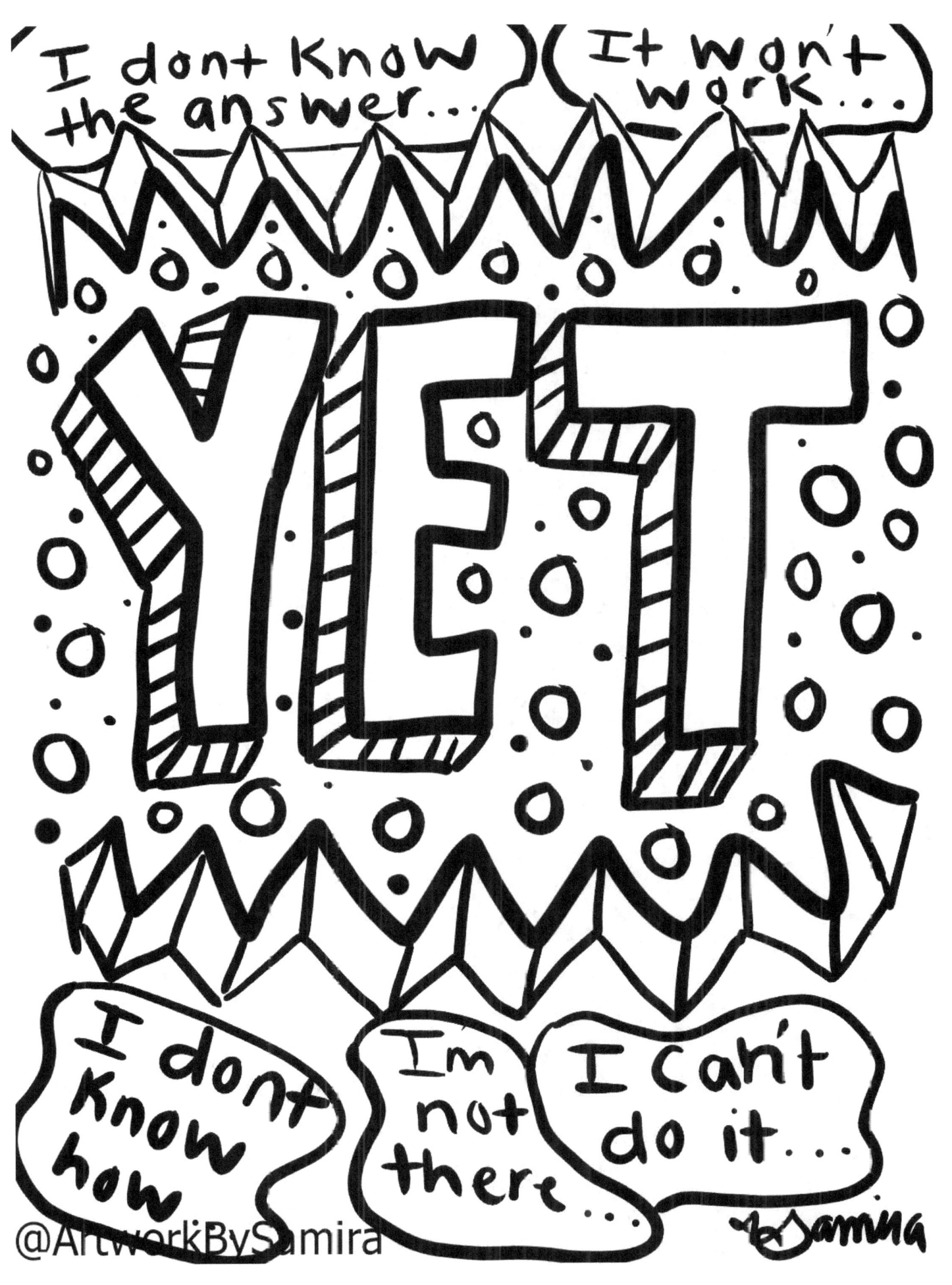

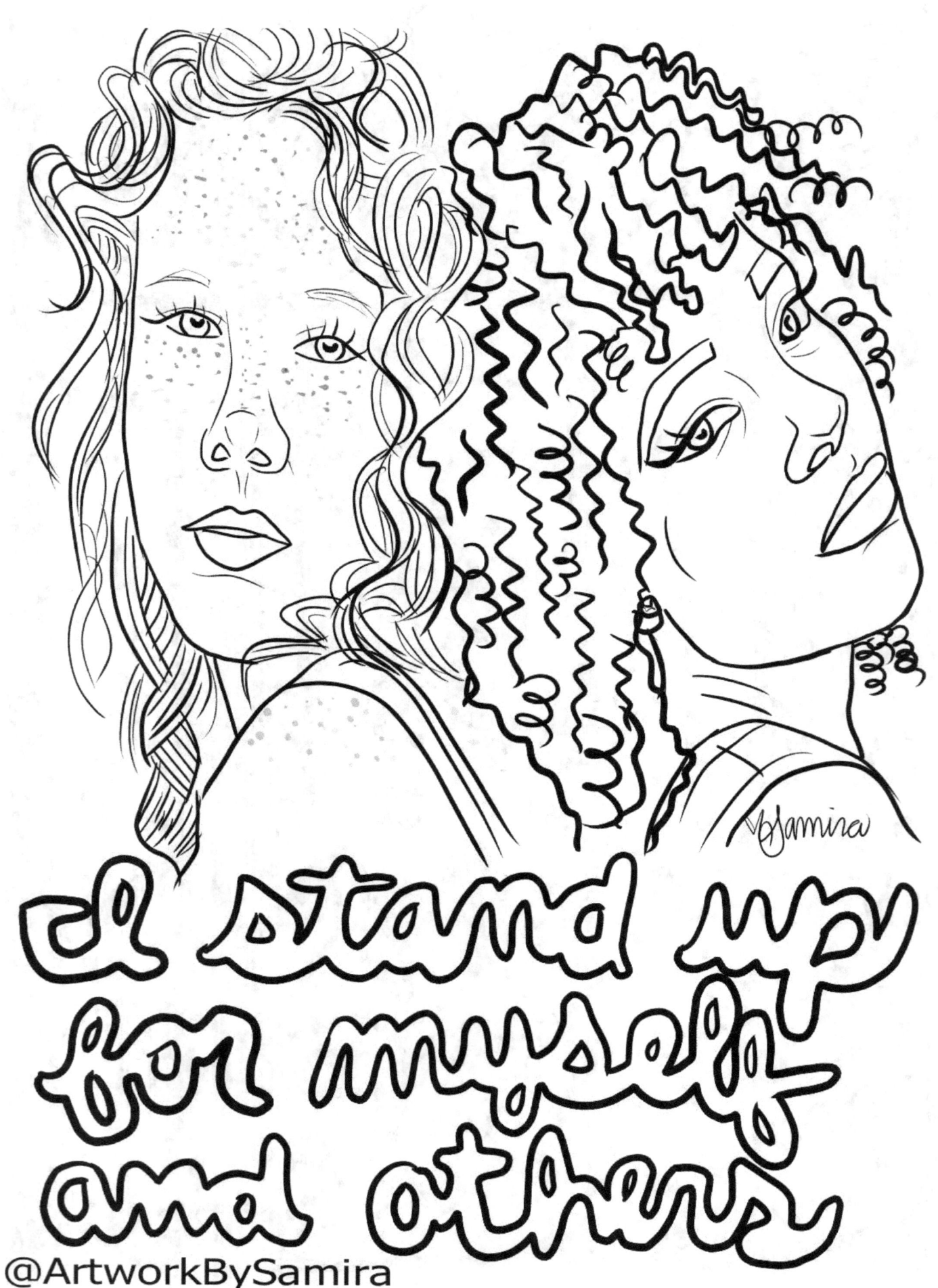

I stand up for myself and others

@ArtworkBySamira

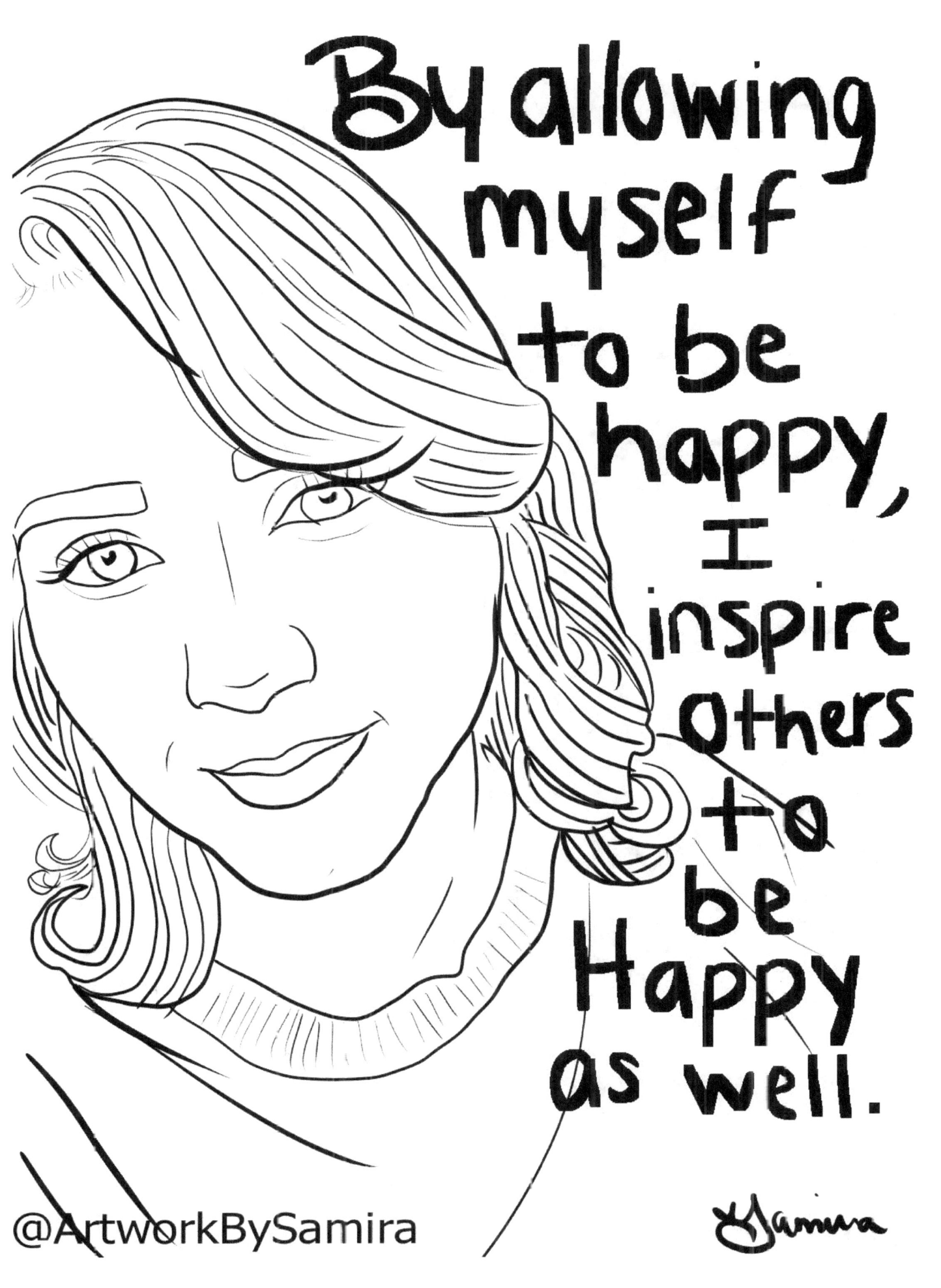

By allowing myself to be happy, I inspire others to be Happy as well.

@ArtworkBySamira

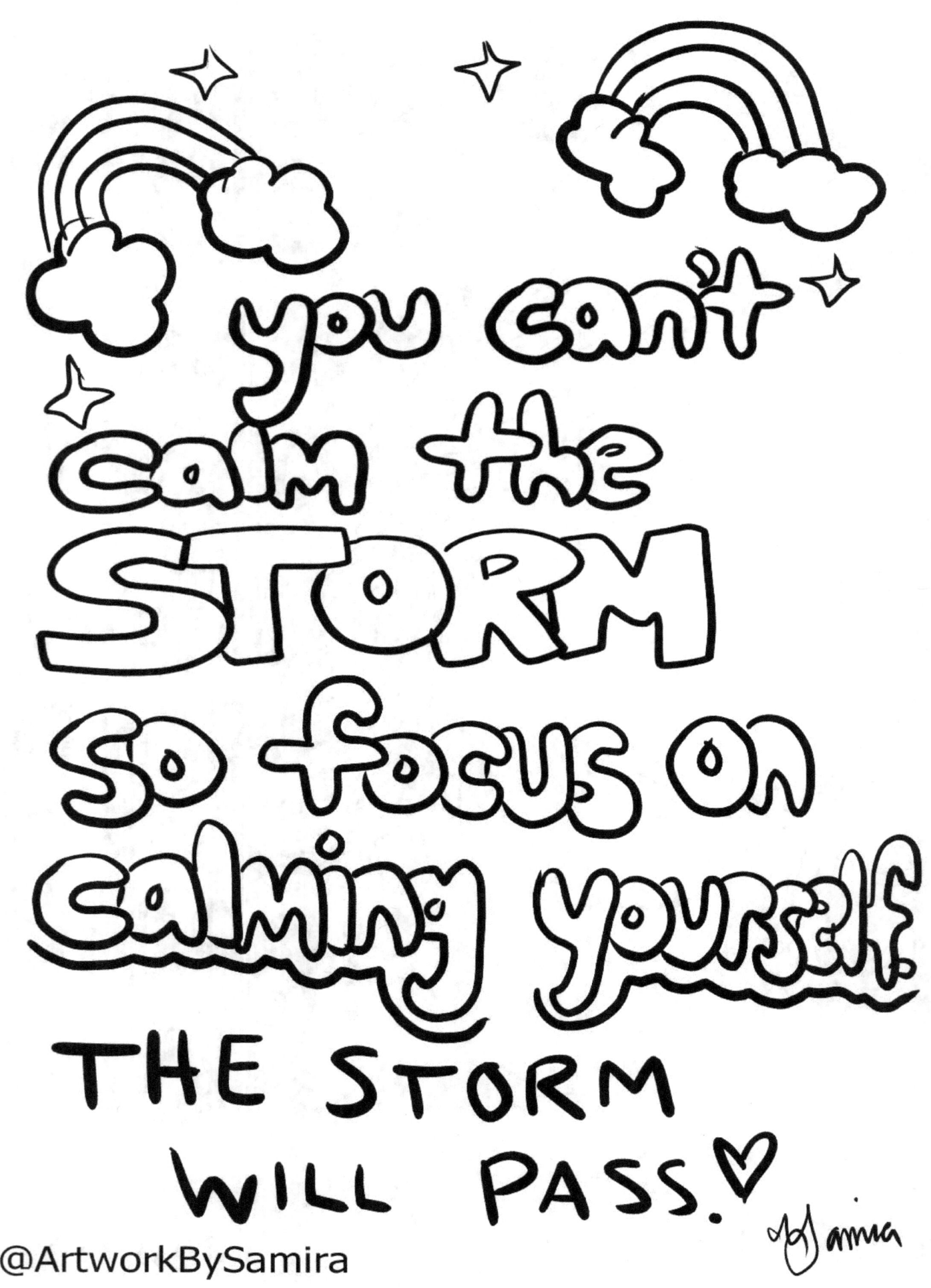

@ArtworkBySamira

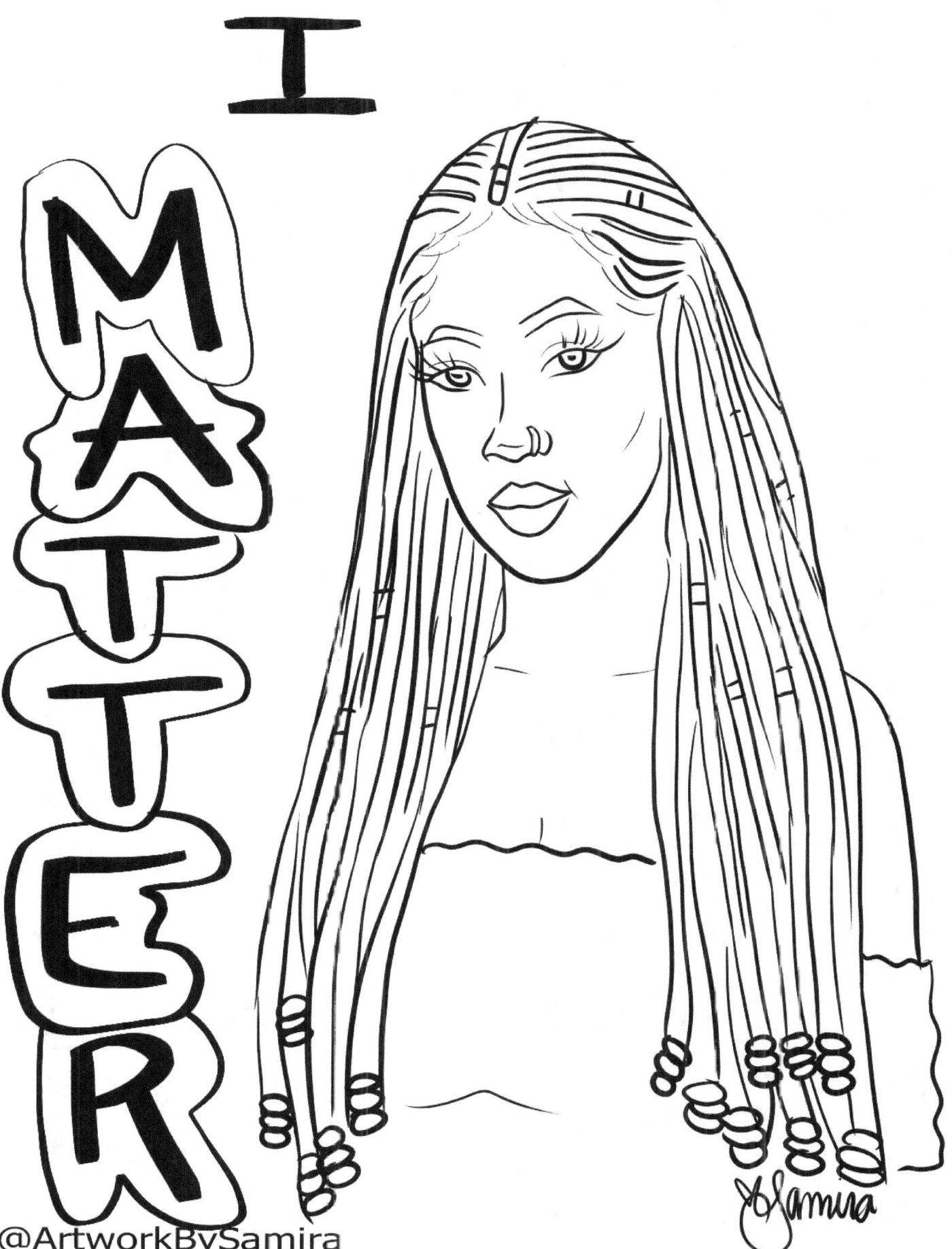

I MATTER

@ArtworkBySamira

Don't let ANYONE tell you you're WEAK because you're a WOMAN

—Mary Kom

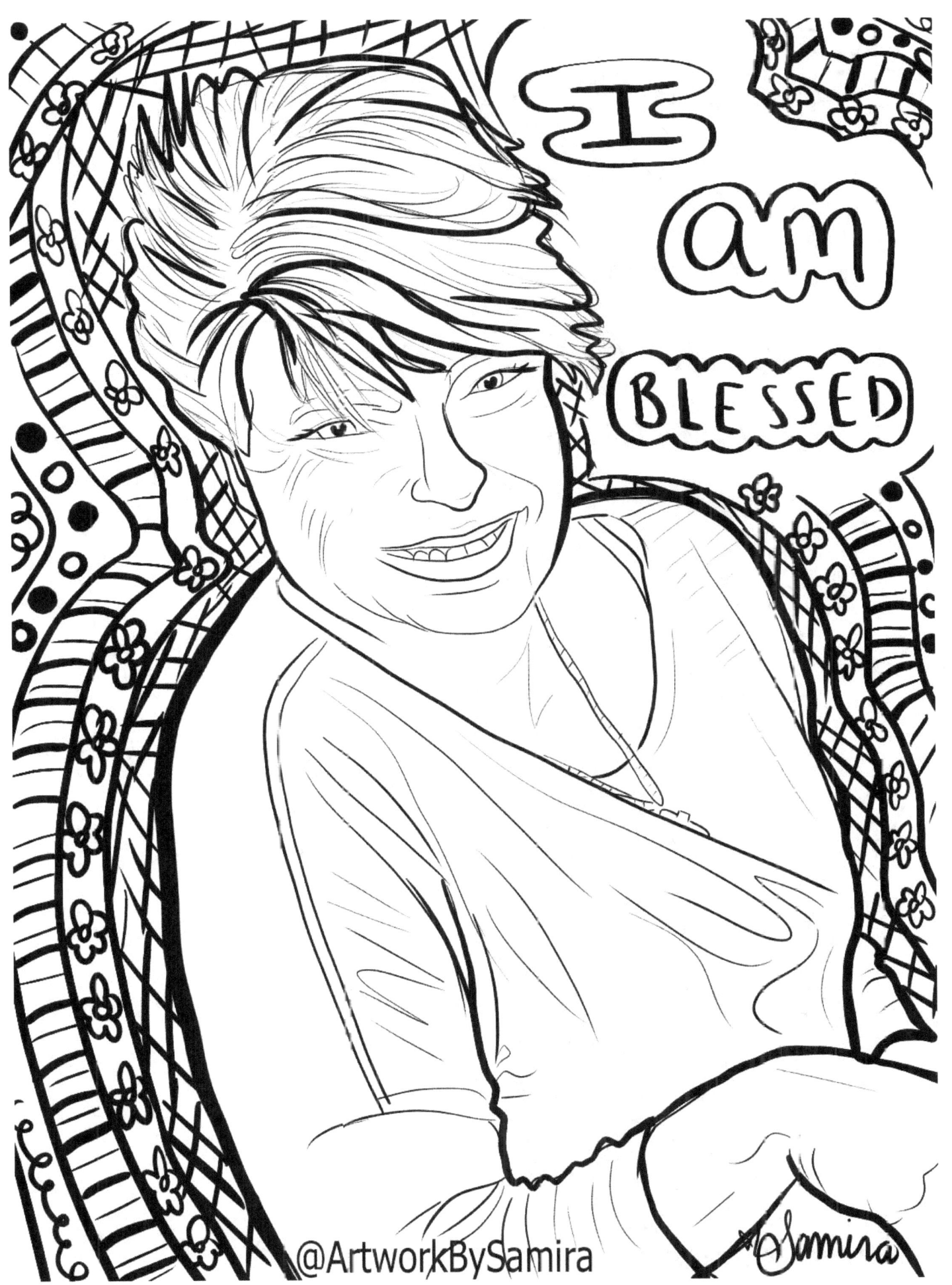

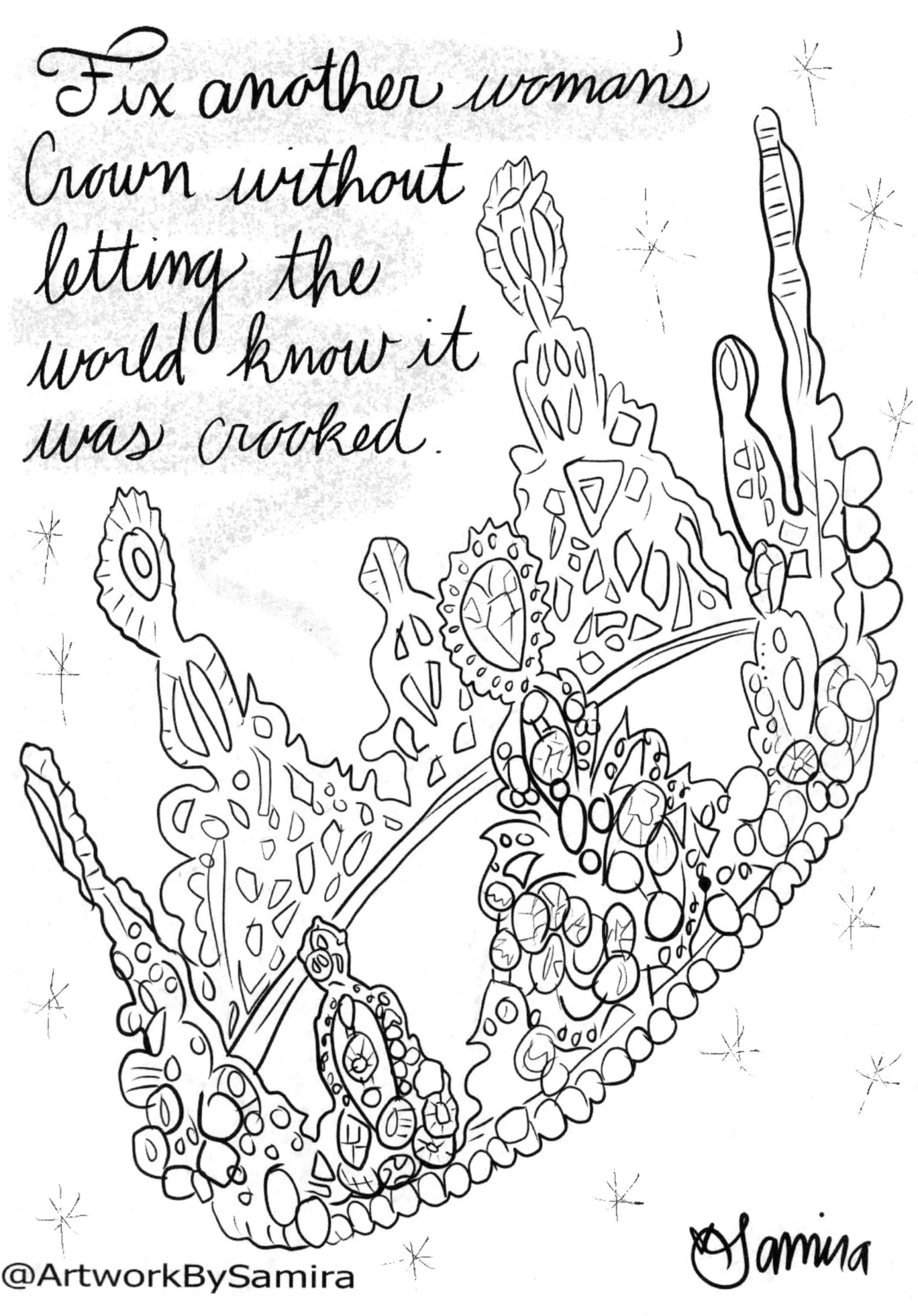

Fix another woman's Crown without letting the world know it was crooked.

Samira

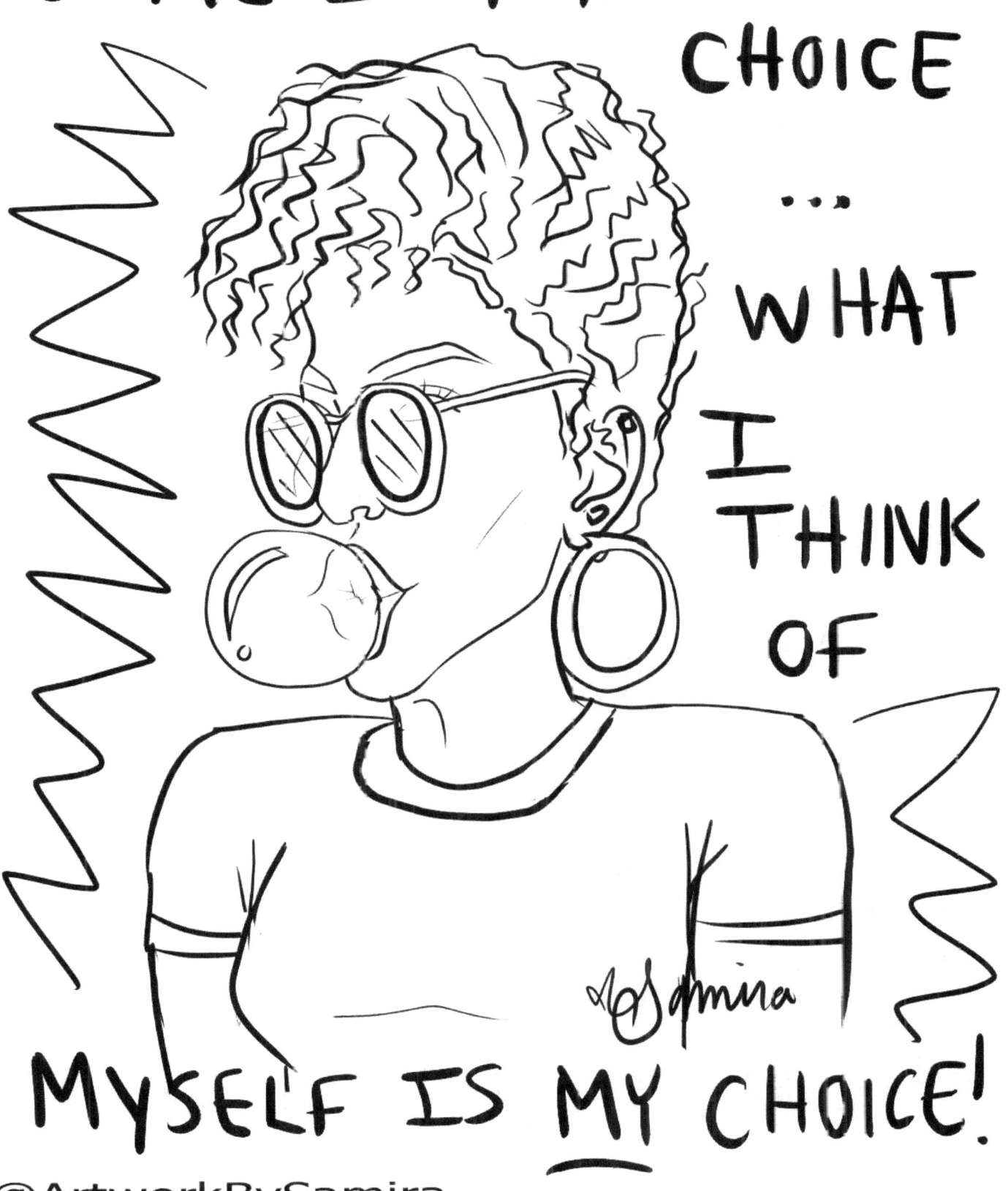

WHAT OTHERS THINK OF ME IS THEIR CHOICE ... WHAT I THINK OF MYSELF IS MY CHOICE!

@ArtworkBySamira

I am curious,

So
I am
always learning

@ArtworkBySamira

EACH TIME

a Woman

STANDS UP

for herself, She Stands up for ♡

ALL WOMEN

@ArtworkBySamira ♡Samira

I AM Beautiful

@ArtworkBySamira

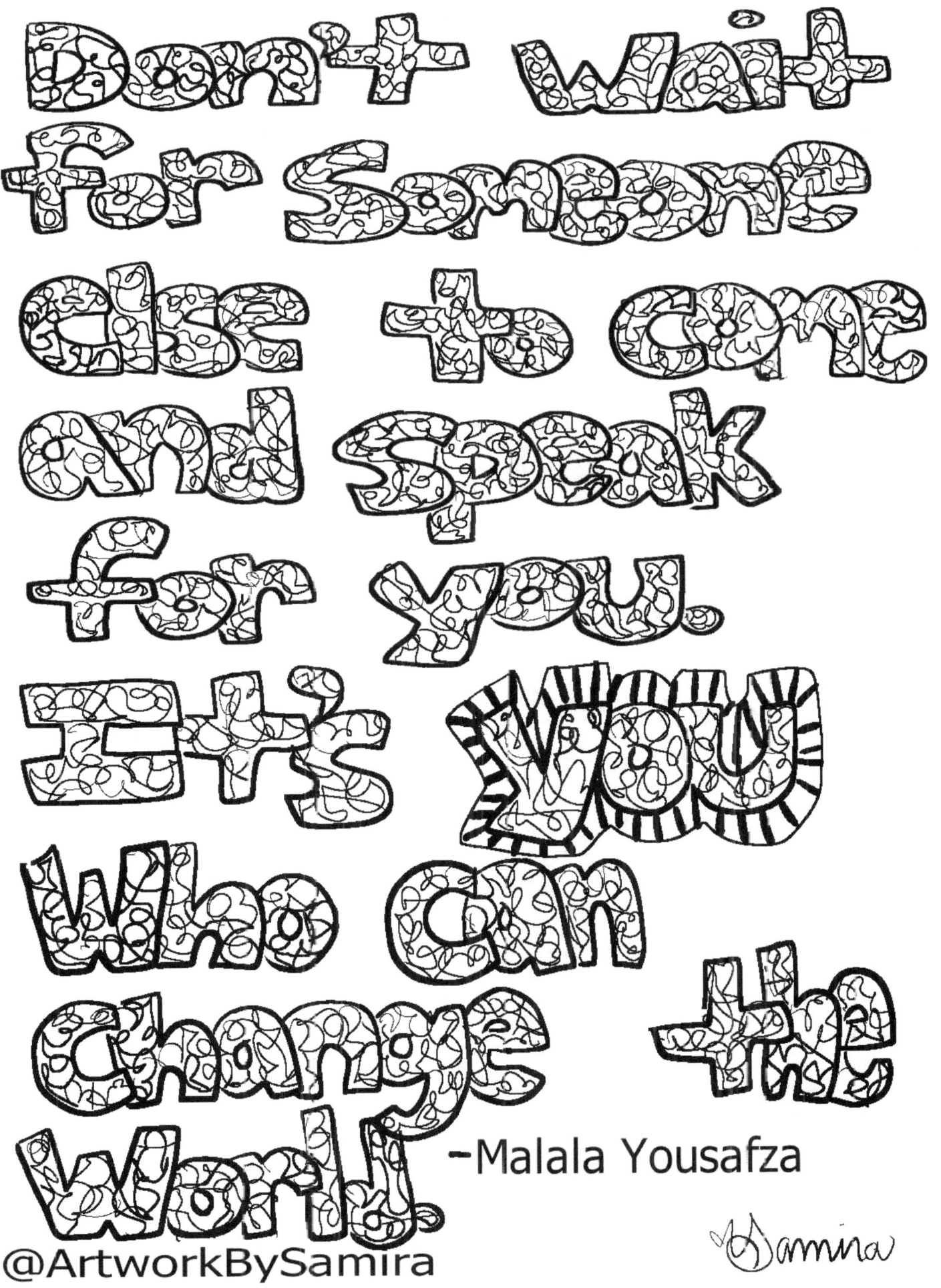

Don't wait for Someone else to come and Speak for you. It's you Who can change the world.

-Malala Yousafza

@ArtworkBySamira

This page is for you! Create your own positive affirmations, and draw a picture.

I am _____

I will_____

I can_____

I _____

www.ingramcontent.com/pod-product-compliance
Lightning Source LLC
Chambersburg PA
CBHW060004230526

45472CB00008B/1937